MY LITTLE

SoHo Kitchen

Dear Ellen,
I hope you like my book.
I'm very lucky to have a
good friend like Christina
to share my foodie travels
Michelle

MY LITTLE

SoHo Kitchen

MICHELLE TCHEA

Marshall Cavendish
Cuisine

Editor: Audrey Yow
Designer: Adithi Khandadi
Food preparation and styling: Michelle Tchea
Photography and styling: Julie Bidwell, Julie Bidwell Photography

Published by Marshall Cavendish Cuisine
An imprint of Marshall Cavendish International

Other Marshall Cavendish Offices:
Marshall Cavendish Corporation. 99 White Plains Road, Tarrytown NY 10591-9001, USA •
Marshall Cavendish International (Thailand) Co Ltd. 253 Asoke, 12th Flr, Sukhumvit 21 Road, Klongtoey Nua,
Wattana, Bangkok 10110, Thailand • Marshall Cavendish (Malaysia) Sdn Bhd, Times Subang, Lot 46,
Subang Hi-Tech Industrial Park, Batu Tiga, 40000 Shah Alam, Selangor Darul Ehsan, Malaysia

Marshall Cavendish is a trademark of Times Publishing Limited

National Library Board, Singapore Cataloguing-in-Publication Data

Tchea, Michelle.
My little SoHo kitchen / Michelle Tchea. -- Singapore : Marshall Cavendish Cuisine, 2013.
pages cm
ISBN : 978-981-4408-62-2 (paperback)

1. Quick and easy cooking. 2. Cooking, Asian. 3. Cooking, American.

TX724.5.A1
641.595 -- dc23   OCN 853014291

Printed in Singapore by KWF Printing Pte Ltd

For Jojo.

Contents

Acknowledgements

My Little SoHo Kitchen is a collection of recipes that capture some of my favourite discoveries and culinary experiences. From simple, timeless classics to new food trends, there are many reasons for me to step into the kitchen. After travelling around and meeting new people in the past year, food has taken on a whole new meaning to me.

To the lovely people who opened up their kitchens and invited me to share a meal at their table, thank you.

To the entire Marshall Cavendish team, thank you for your support and for giving me an opportunity to share more recipes and food experiences.

To Audrey, my editor, thank you for your friendly emails and encouraging words. I appreciate all your time and help.

To Julie, my photographer, thank you for your time and for sharing the East Coast culture with me.

To my favourite kitchen brands, thank you for the support and for sharing my excitement. To the wonderful team at Villeroy and Boch, you have brightened up my home with your beautiful tableware. I definitely feel part of the family now. Emile Henry, thank you for giving me a bit of France in New York with your lovely cookware. Laura Ashley, thank you for the gorgeous linens and my favourite apron. Cuisinart, thank you for confirming my belief that your products are essential for all cooks. Joseph Joseph Kitchenware, I'm a chemist in my kitchen with your innovative tools. NuNu Chocolates in Brooklyn — deliciously addictive. Stew Leonards and Fairway Markets — my favourite places to shop when I can't get to a farm. A big thank you to Lockworks at Yale and Towne — the photoshoot wouldn't be the same without your help.

To my family, the eight most important people in my life, thank you for your invaluable support. Family BBQs, morning coffees and dramas at the table can never be replaced.

Jojo, thanks for bragging to all your friends about my first book, *Building a Perfect Meal*. You inspired me to keep going. Thank you for all the bacon-stuffed baked potatoes, Timezone games and encouraging hugs … of course I am thinking of you.

Introduction

Sitting on the kitchen counter watching my mum and aunt make dumplings by hand are my earliest memories. Growing up, I was spoiled rotten by lunchboxes filled with more than just chips and sandwiches, but I traded my mum's Taiwanese spring onion pancakes for Aussie vegemite sandwiches at school. I tried to disguise my background and did not understand why my mum packed such elaborate lunches, when all I wanted was a boring sandwich like the one in my friend's lunchbox. Fortunately, growing up and travelling around have given me the palette and curiosity to appreciate different cuisines and cultures. Diversity is what makes cooking exciting.

My Little SoHo Kitchen is not just for those living in New York. It is for everyone out there who wants to make fuss-free, good food in the home kitchen. The recipes in this book are inspired by friends and neighbours, and they are not too complicated even for a last-minute weekday meal. Some were created in my petit kitchen in Switzerland, others while I was a chemist in Japan — my tiniest kitchen ever! I even have a handful of recipes that I can and sometimes do use in a hotel room. So on days when you crave food that you can't simply get from across the street, pop into your kitchen and whip up something great. Don't let the restrictions of a small kitchen or the lack of fancy kitchen tools deter you. I can use a rice cooker to steam fish, poach eggs or boil beans. If I can't find a whisk, I use a fork. A blowtorch can work as well as an oven for toasting marshmallows. Just because I have a small kitchen doesn't mean I can't have fun.

The great thing about cooking is that you don't have to follow recipes to the tee — rather, use ingredients that you feel will work, or simply use whatever you have on hand. I have tried to keep the recipes simple and versatile, and it is my hope that this book can be a source of inspiration with every turn of a page.

Inspirations and Ideas

I love creating meals that are a little out of the ordinary. Not only does this give me the flexibility to quash all expectations when the dish doesn't turn out quite like the picture in the book, but it also gives me the chance to cook on a whim, using ingredients that are on hand for a simple, yet totally delicious meal. When it comes to cooking, I like to keep things simple. So, as much as I love food, I don't like spending too much time in the kitchen.

Having seen many cookbooks, food magazines and online foodzines, I didn't want to churn out another book with the same recipes you can find off the shelf. With celebrity chefs, famous cooks and food bloggers changing the way we see food, I want to write a book that collates everyday recipes with a touch of creativity. Nothing too complicated, I like to leave that to the experts, just recipes that can feed a growling stomach.

I've picked my favourite recipes that combine memories from fantastic dining experiences, great flavours from seasonal ingredients as well as techniques learnt during my childhood. *My little SoHo kitchen* does have its limits, but my culinary imagination is definitely unrestricted.

Farmers Markets

Having a huge passion for fresh fruit and local produce, I was concerned about moving to a big city.

I don't like buying supermarket produce with long expiration dates, or having to enlist the help of friends from surrounding states to ship fresh food from local producers and farmers for me. Luckily, New York being New York, demands are always met here. Suburban life comes to the city with independent growers setting up community gardens in the heart of Manhattan. From herb gardens on rooftops to vegetable patches sprouting up throughout the five boroughs, there is nothing you can't find in New York. But for those without a green thumb, the farmers markets are definitely my pick for fresh produce. I can get fresh fish from the seafood vender in Union Square without having to travel to Connecticut for the fresh catch of the day. Apples can be purchased in bags — perfect for desserts and home-made sweets without feeling guilty of over-indulgence.

It's a bit of France in the heart of a busy city — I love it!

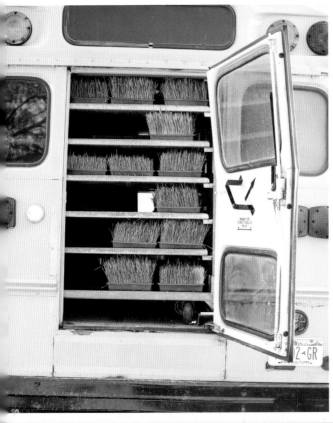

Living, Cooking and Eating in New York

As an Aussie in a big city, I get quite excited when I spot stars in a café. It's like I am part of a sitcom or movie. And since this book is a compilation of my SoHo experiences, with some inspiration from my travels around Europe, I feel that each chapter is like an episode of a drama serial that I will never get tired of watching.

When I first moved to New York, I experienced a few very New York-y moments. I jumped into a yellow cab, wound down the window and stuck my head out breathing in the city air while cruising across George Washington Bridge. To me, New York isn't about dining in high-end restaurants or making reservations at bistros trending in the magazines. It's about the food joints that line each street corner in a city that never sleeps. Pizzas in the Lower West Village, bagels in the Upper East, Taiwanese food in Flushing … what else could a self-professed food tragic want?

I haven't quite managed to kick my naughty food habits in New York, but I can proudly say that I am improving in the way I eat, live and cook as a New Yorker. Having tried all the noteworthy pubs, restaurants and cafés lining the streets of Upper Manhattan, I consistently feel the draw of the artistry scene that New Yorkers officially call SoHo.

Bounded by major streets in Manhattan — Houston, Lafayette and Canal — the South of Houston Street, or SoHo, as it is commonly referred to, is a world of its own. High priced lofts that were once home to many artists are now homes to famous celebrities and TV personalities — a far cry from the struggling artists that used the open lofts as inspiration. Surrounding neighbourhoods are rougher in Chinatown and the vibrant Italian district known as NoLita (North of Little Italy). The Meat-packing district and the TriBeCa (Triangle Below Canal Street) area are places I tend to go to, as the pebble stones and slightly less tourist-populated areas promise better places to sit and enjoy a slice of pizza.

These typical scenes are unique to the SoHo neighbourhood: Well-dressed model-like girls sitting outside sipping coffee, fanny-packed tourists darting in and out of boutiques for a bargain, and workers moving shipments of paintings and artwork in and out of the cast-iron lofts.

The hip and popular environment of SoHo makes it a great place for food lovers. It is central to many of the best restaurants in the city, and creating recipes in a neighbourhood home to many independent artists gives me fuel to revolutionise the way people eat. The SoHo Effect that has influenced the way New Yorkers live has slightly changed the way I cook in my little SoHo kitchen.

Although I have a more creative and vibrant lifestyle as a SoHo-lite, I have traded in my open spaced kitchen for a tiny one that almost feels like an airplane cabin. Living in Japan trained me to make the most of tiny spaces, so a small kitchen definitely doesn't restrict me. You just have to draw inspiration from the artists of SoHo and the chefs of New York, and come up with delicious recipes that satisfy cravings.

My favourite moment during the day is when it's bright and early, when the streets of New York are almost silent and all the tourists are still tucked nicely in their hotel beds. Waking up to the sun peeking into my window, I jump out of my bed and hit the New York pavement in search of breakfast. There's nothing better than walking up and down the streets of New York, watching the city slowly getting ready for another day of feeding locals, entertaining tourists and living up to expectations.

Episode 1

Simple Dinners

When I decided to move to the East Coast of the US, I wasn't worried about packing my whole life in a tiny apartment and braving the snow during winter, but gaining the US travel pounds and getting fat! With all the food choices available at my door step and the convenience of the New York lifestyle, I wondered if I would ever cook in my tiny SoHo kitchen. The SoHo neighbourhood offers some fun brunch places and great cafés to sit and watch New Yorkers go by. However, stepping out of my box and venturing to the Upper East and West opens a whole new world of amazing food.

Luckily, with great markets popping up in the city and nearby farms in the Tri-State area, I soon found excuses to eat at home. Although I welcome every chance to explore the side streets and restaurants dotted around Manhattan and beyond, there is something very comforting about a well-stocked fridge and cooking at home. Using simple ingredients, delicious dishes can be created with little effort.

Quick and easy meals can be made from frozen bags of minced meat for super quick meatballs, as well as frozen corn and peas that are great additions to jazz up any meal. Farm fresh eggs and frozen semi-cooked beans are staples in my kitchen, as are noodles, rice and mixed grains. These are just some of the things that make my life easier should I decide to cook on a whim.

Spicy Meatballs in Rich Tomato Sauce

Makes about 18 meatballs

Pork sausage 100 g (3$\frac{1}{2}$ oz)

Ground pork 200 g (7 oz)

Ground beef 200 g (7 oz)

Dried oregano 1 tsp

Paprika $\frac{1}{2}$ tsp

Lemon zest $\frac{1}{2}$ tsp

Dijon mustard 1 tsp

Fresh breadcrumbs 50 g (1$\frac{2}{3}$ oz)

Salt to taste

Ground white pepper to taste

Olive oil 2 Tbsp

Onion 1, peeled and finely diced

Garlic 2 cloves, peeled and quartered

Tomato Sauce

Red wine 125 ml (4 fl oz / $\frac{1}{2}$ cup)

Tomatoes 500 g (1 lb 1$\frac{1}{2}$ oz)

Onion 1, peeled and sliced

Garlic 3 cloves, peeled and finely chopped

Tomato paste 1 tsp

Fresh basil a handful

Chilli flakes 1 tsp, or 1 tsp Korean spice paste

Worcestershire sauce 1 tsp

1. Remove sausage casing. Using your hands, loosen the mixture to break up the meat chunks in a large mixing bowl.

2. Add ground pork and beef to sausage meat. Combine meats by squeezing the mixture gently between your fingers while moving the meat around the bowl.

3. When well mixed, make a small well in the centre and add oregano, paprika, lemon zest and Dijon mustard. Continue to mix until well combined. For tender, juicy meatballs, gather handfuls of meat and throw them against the side of the bowl repeatedly for a minute or two, until it becomes more sticky.

4. Add breadcrumbs. Sprinkle salt and pepper, keeping in mind that the sausages are already seasoned. If you have time and your stomach isn't growling too furiously, set aside in the fridge for at least 25 minutes to let the flavours develop. Otherwise, divide the mixture in half, then in half again. Continue to halve each ball of mixture until each of them is the desired meatball size. Place meatballs on a clean tray until ready to use.

5. Heat oil in a heavy cast iron or ceramic pot. When oil is hot, sear meatballs in batches until they are a nice golden colour. This helps to lock in the juices. Toss the meatballs until they turn brown on the outside, and pink on the inside. Repeat for remaining batches of meatballs. Set cooked meatballs aside.

6. Using the same pot, use remaining oil to sauté onion and garlic until aromatic.

7. Prepare tomato sauce. Add red wine to deglaze the pot, gently scraping off the caramelised meat from the bottom of the pot with a wooden spoon. Add remaining ingredients. Add a splash of water, about 125 ml (4 fl oz / $\frac{1}{2}$ cup), if it looks a little dry. Bring to the boil and reduce to a simmer.

8. Add in meatballs and continue to simmer for about 20 minutes.

9. If desired, season with salt and pepper before serving.

Minced meat is an excellent ingredient to use. It is cheap, flavourful and a fast-cooking ingredient. Use minced meat with some fat as it produces more natural juices when cooked. This recipe uses sausages for extra flavour — a quick fix instead of leaving the meat to marinate while your stomach growls with hunger.

Saucy Mac 'n' Cheese

Serves 4

Macaroni 250 g (9 oz)

Egg 1

Milk 250 ml (8 fl oz / 1 cup)

Ground nutmeg a sprinkle

Ground black pepper to taste

Gruyère cheese 140 g (5 oz) grated + 45 g (1^1/$_2$ oz), cubed

Cheddar cheese 85 g (3 oz), grated

Mozzarella cheese 85 g (3 oz), grated

Mascarpone cheese 4 Tbsp

Cherry tomatoes 6, halved

Panko breadcrumbs 150 g (5^1/$_3$ oz)

Butter 2 Tbsp, cubed

1. Preheat oven to 160°C (325°F).

2. Bring a large pot of water to the boil. Add macaroni and cook for about 7 minutes. Drain macaroni and reserve about 125 ml (4 fl oz / ^{1}/$_2$ cup) of the liquid. Set aside.

3. In another bowl, crack egg into milk. Sprinkle in nutmeg and add a dash of pepper. Add Gruyère, Cheddar and Mozzarella cheese. Stir to combine.

4. Throw in semi-cooked macaroni and its reserved liquid. Mix evenly.

5. Stir in Mascarpone cheese, then pour everything into a lightly greased rectangular baking dish. Top with cherry tomatoes.

6. Sprinkle breadcrumbs and arrange cubed butter evenly on top.

7. Bake for 45 minutes to 1 hour, until the top is brown and crusty.

8. Serve warm.

My perfect Mac 'n' Cheese has a thick sauce with bullets of cheese dotted throughout. After living in Switzerland and eating copious amounts of cheese, I was inspired to revamp an old favourite. Regular Mac 'n' Cheese recipes seem complicated and use far too many pots and pans for such a simple comfort food. This is my cheat version that doesn't require béchamel sauce, yet still gives a delicious, creamy bake. The combination of three different cheeses gives that glossy, gooey cheese sauce that will satisfy anytime.

Crispy Pork Cutlet with Salad

Serves 2

Pork cutlets or loins 2, about 1 cm (½-in) thick

Plain (all-purpose) flour 2 heaped Tbsp

Egg 1, beaten and combined with 4 Tbsp buttermilk

Panko breadcrumbs 150 g (5⅓ oz)

Cooking oil for deep-frying

Salad

Carrots 2, peeled and shredded into slivers

Coriander 4 Tbsp, freshly chopped

Ground black pepper a sprinkle

Vinaigrette

Wholegrain mustard 1 tsp

Sherry or white vinegar 1–2 Tbsp

Small shallot 1, peeled and finely diced

Olive oil 3 Tbsp

Dill 1 tsp, finely chopped

1. Combine all ingredients for vinaigrette, adjusting amounts for Sherry or white vinegar to taste. Set aside.

2. Prepare salad in a mixing bowl. Mix carrots and coriander, then sprinkle pepper. Drizzle vinaigrette over and toss to mix well.

3. Lightly prick pork cutlets with a fork on both sides, then dredge. Lightly coat each cutlet in flour before dipping into the egg and buttermilk mixture. Then, roll pork into breadcrumbs until evenly coated. Remove excess dredging ingredients as you go along to prevent clumps from forming. If a thicker batter is preferred, dip pork into egg and buttermilk mixture, followed by breadcrumbs, for a second time. Set aside on a tray.

4. Heat oil to about 170°C (338°F). Slowly lower one pork cutlet into the oil with clean, dry tongs. Flip to get an even browning on both sides. Cook for 5–6 minutes. Increase to high heat 1 minute before removing from oil to get a nice crust. To check if it is well cooked, cut into the thickest part, and it should be opaque and firm. Set aside on a wire rack to drain off oil.

5. Bring oil temperature back up to 170°C (338°F) before repeating the deep-frying process for the other cutlet.

6. While waiting for the oil to drain off from the cutlets, arrange salad on serving plates.

7. Arrange pork cutlets alongside salad. If desired, serve with Tonkatsu or barbecue sauce.

Note: I prefer to deep-fry rather than pan-fry pork cutlets because it gives a more even coating, and the meat juices are better locked in. If you prefer to pan-fry the cutlets, fill the pan with oil, up to about 0.5 cm (¼ in) in height. Heat oil to about 180°C (350°F) to fry each cutlet. To test the temperature of the oil, drop in a small cube of bread into heated oil. If it sizzles, the oil is ready for use.

I always think of a perfect summer lunch when I make this dish. Serve with a simple salad or have it sandwiched between soft white bread. Many countries have their own versions of this dish, and I have gathered my favourite cooking techniques and flavours to make this my own.

Chilli and Garlic Squid on Rice

Serves 2

Fresh squid 500 g (1 lb 1¹/₂ oz)

Peanut oil 2 Tbsp

Onion 1, peeled and sliced

Garlic 2 cloves, peeled and finely chopped

Ground cumin ¹/₂ tsp

Red chilli 1, deseeded

Chilli paste 1 tsp

Brown sugar 1 tsp

Large celery stick 1, thinly sliced

Red pepper (capsicum) ¹/₂, sliced

Spring onions (scallions) 2, chopped into 2.5-cm (1-in) lengths

Salt to taste

Toasted peanuts for garnishing

1. Clean squid under cold running water. Remove head and tentacles. Pull out the backbone (quill) and wash the inside of the cavity. Drain in a colander.

2. Halve squid lengthwise such that it lies flat. Cut into pieces of desired size. Score criss cross patterns on the insides of the squid pieces, as this allows the squid to curl up nicely when cooked. Alternatively, simply cut squid into strips.

3. Heat 1 Tbsp oil in a pan. When oil is hot enough, stir-fry onion and garlic until onion is translucent. Add cumin, chilli, chilli paste and sugar. Cook until fragrant. Add celery and red pepper. Continue to sauté for about 2 minutes, until slightly cooked and still crunchy.

4. Push ingredients to the side of the pan. Heat remaining 1 Tbsp oil to cook squid. After about 45 seconds, when squid changes from opaque to white and curls up, add spring onions and season with salt. Remove from heat.

5. Garnish with toasted peanuts and serve with steamed rice.

Note: Squid should either be cooked very quickly or very slowly. For a quick and simple meal, do not cook the squid for more than a minute. To ensure everything goes smoothly, it's best to have everything prepared before starting to cook this dish.

Squid is fantastic for quick dinners because it takes just seconds to cook. I like the classic combination of chilli and squid, and will tend to add lots of chillies. Feel free to play around with the chilli amounts to your liking.

Salmon with Egg Tapenade

Serves 2

Salmon fillets 2, scaled, skin retained
Asparagus spears several, grilled
Cherry tomatoes a handful, halved
Pesto sauce (see page 56) 1 Tbsp

Pickle Dressing
White vinegar 500 ml (16 fl oz / 2 cups)
Sugar 2 Tbsp
Water 125 ml (4 fl oz / ¹/₂ cup)
Black peppercorns 8, slightly crushed
Bay leaf 1
Salt 1 Tbsp

Egg Tapenade
Eggs 4
Mayonnaise 2 Tbsp
Sour cream 1 Tbsp
Capers 1 tsp
Small onion 1, finely chopped
Salt a pinch
Ground black pepper a pinch

1. In a pot, bring all ingredients for pickle dressing to the boil. Allow to cool completely.

2. Wash fish fillets under cold running water and pat dry. Place on a shallow baking tray and pour over pickle dressing. Refrigerate for at least 25 minutes, which will give the salmon a sashimi-like centre and a soft, poached outer crust. The longer the fish is pickled, the more cured it will be.

3. Prepare egg tapenade. Submerge eggs in room temperature water and bring to the boil. Simmer on medium heat for about 6 minutes, until the yolks are just cooked through. Immediately plunge into cold water for about 5 minutes.

4. Peel the eggs, separating the yolks and the whites. Dice egg whites. Mash egg yolks with mayonnaise and sour cream before combining with capers, onion and egg whites. Season with salt and pepper.

5. Drain pickled salmon in a colander to remove excess liquid.

6. Heat oil in a small pan and sear salmon fillets, skin side down, for about 30 seconds, until the skin is crispy and brown.

7. Serve with asparagus, cherry tomatoes and pesto sauce.

This is a great dish for a lazy afternoon over the weekend, accompanied by a good bottle of wine. The longer you cure the fish, the more cooked it will be. Be sure to use the freshest, high quality sashimi-grade salmon available. I like this served with grilled asparagus and sweet cherry tomatoes — one of my favourite lunches.

Episode 2

One-dish Meals

Although I was born and raised in Australia, my Chinese background dictates all my movements in the kitchen and at the table. My mum makes huge portions, enough to feed the entire lower east side of Manhattan. Surprisingly, there are never any leftovers. When I first moved out, I found it difficult to cook for one and never really got the hang of it. Luckily, my mum gave me some good advice and suggested recipes that could last for two days. In fact, recipes like Chicken with Braised Beans and Peas are even better the following night after re-heating. Savoury Seafood Rice and Beer-steamed Mussels are incredibly easy and are best eaten immediately. Something tells me there won't be any leftovers after you've tasted them.

Savoury Seafood Rice

Serves 2–3

Olive oil for frying

Onion 1, peeled and sliced

Garlic 2 cloves, peeled and sliced

Red pepper (capsicum) $1/2$, deseeded and sliced

Chorizo sausage 1, broken into pieces

Paprika 1 tsp

Mussels 250 g (9 oz), shells intact, washed and cleaned

Mix of calamari and prawns (shrimps) 300 g ($10^1/_2$ oz)

Any paella rice or Arborio 200 g (7 oz)

Salt to taste

Ground black pepper to taste

Fish stock 500 ml (16 fl oz / 2 cups)

Green peas 75 g ($2^2/_3$ oz)

Fresh parsley a few sprigs

Lemon wedges a few

1. Heat oil over medium to high heat in a large casserole dish with a fitted lid. Sauté onion and garlic until onion is translucent and the sweet juices are released. Add red pepper and cook until it wilts with the onions.

2. Add chorizo and paprika. Break up the chorizo and continue to cook. Add half the mussels and the mix of calamari and prawns. Shake the pan to mix well.

3. Add rice, salt and pepper, fish stock and peas. Give the pan a final gentle jiggle and make sure the liquid is at least 1.5 cm ($3/_4$ in) above all the ingredients.

4. Place remaining mussels on top before putting on the lid.

5. Bring to a low boil, before reducing to a simmer. Allow to simmer for 16–20 minutes, until the mussels have opened up and the rice is cooked through.

6. Garnish with fresh parsley and lemon wedges before serving.

Spanish paella is a combination of plump fluffy rice and fresh seafood in a fragrant broth. There are a lot of rules to making paella, which can make the dish quite elaborate. According to my chef friends in Spain, you need fresh ingredients, the right mix of spices and of course, the perfect paella rice. Wanting to eat this without all the hard work, this is my spin on a dish that doesn't require you to stand over the stove and watch it like a hawk. The perfect paella should never be stirred, but simply jiggled to fluff up the rice. It is normal for the rice at the top to be slightly undercooked and for a golden crust known as socarrat to form at the base of the pan. If you have all these, consider yourself a paella expert.

Chicken with Braised Beans and Peas

Serves 2–3

Chicken drumsticks or thighs 500 g (1 lb 1½ oz), about 4 pieces, skinned

Pancetta 4–6 rashers

Olive oil for frying

Onion 1, peeled and chopped

Garlic 2 cloves, peeled and finely chopped

Leek 1 stalk, preferably white part with a bit of green

Ground black pepper a pinch

Vegetable stock 375 ml (12 fl oz / 1½ cups)

Asparagus spears 12, ends snapped and roughly chopped in half

Green peas 300 g (10½ oz)

White beans 425 g (15 oz), semi-cooked

Pesto sauce (see page 56) 1 Tbsp

Lemon wedge 1

1. Rinse chicken pieces under cold running water and pat dry with a paper towel.

2. Wrap each chicken piece with a rasher of pancetta.

3. Heat oil over medium heat in a pan. When the oil is hot, add wrapped chicken and lightly fry on all sides until golden brown. Remove chicken from heat and set aside.

4. In the same pan, add another 1 Tbsp oil and sauté onion and garlic for 1 minute. Add leek and continue to cook for another minute. Sprinkle in some pepper.

5. Pour in just enough stock so that it is just a little over the leeks. Add chicken pieces and put on the lid. Simmer for about 20 minutes, until leeks have collapsed and the chicken pieces are cooked through.

6. Add asparagus, peas and white beans before giving it a good stir. Stir in pesto sauce. Cook for a further 5–8 minutes until vegetables and beans are cooked.

7. Remove from heat and serve with a lemon wedge.

I love spring purely for its abundance of fresh vegetables. The combination of peas, white beans and asparagus is a delicious mix of spring in a bowl. Paired with chicken wrapped in a salty cured meat such as pancetta, this dish makes a delightful indulgence. I prefer to use semi-cooked beans rather than canned ones, since braising the beans keeps the pulses in shape.

Pork Sausage Angel Hair Pasta

Serves 1

Angel hair pasta 80–100 g (2$^4/_5$–3$^1/_2$ oz)

Olive oil 1 Tbsp

Butter 1 Tbsp

Garlic 2 cloves, peeled and finely chopped

Capers 1 Tbsp

Sage leaves 3

Good-quality pork sausage 1

Red pepper (capsicum) $^1/_2$, finely sliced

Parsley leaves a good handful, roughly chopped

1. Bring water to a boil in a large pot. Cook pasta according to package instructions.

2. Heat oil and butter in a pan. Once the butter melts, fry garlic, capers and sage until they are a nice golden colour. Add sausage, breaking it up with the back of your spatula into bite sizes. Add red pepper.

3. When pasta is ready, drain and reserve about 4 Tbsp of its cooking liquid.

4. Add pasta to the sausage mixture in the pan and give it a quick toss. Add reserved pasta cooking liquid if it looks a little dry.

5. Stir in parsley leaves, remove from heat and serve.

Good-quality sausages are full of flavour and are extremely versatile. Apart from just filling a hotdog bun, sausage meat can also be used for pastas, casseroles and potato bakes. Invest in good-quality sausages for this dish, and I promise the delicate and fragrant juices from the meat will be perfect for this satisfying meal.

Wild Mushrooms with Blue Cheese and Thyme

Serves 2

Butter 1 Tbsp + more for spreading

Garlic 1 clove, peeled and finely chopped

Fresh thyme a few leaves, finely chopped

Mixed wild mushrooms 200 g (7 oz)

Salt a sprinkle

Ground black pepper a sprinkle

Blue cheese 50 g (1²/₃ oz), crumbled

1. Melt butter in a heated pan. Sauté garlic and fresh thyme until aromatic.

2. Add mushrooms. Toss until the mushrooms start to collapse, but have not released its juices yet. If using chanterelles, allow to char a little so that there's more flavour.

3. Stir in salt and pepper. Turn off heat and add blue cheese. Toss until the cheese melts a little from the residual heat.

4. Serve with toasted rustic bread and a liberal spread of butter.

Note: Use mushrooms of your choice, such as cremini, chanterelle, shiitake, brown mushrooms, etc.

Wild mushrooms are delicious when mixed with fresh herbs and butter. To clean mushrooms, use a moist towel and give them a good wipe to get rid of dirt. A final tip: cook your mushrooms quickly so that the natural juices remain in the mushrooms rather than in your pan.

Beer-steamed Mussels

Serves 2

Olive oil for frying

Garlic 2 cloves, peeled and minced

Onion 1, peeled and diced

Mussels 500 g (1 lb 1½ oz), cleaned

Dijon mustard 1 heaped tsp

Beer 125 ml (4 fl oz / ½ cup)

Single (light) cream (optional) 2 Tbsp

Fresh parsley a generous handful, shredded

1. Heat oil in a heavy saucepan. Stir-fry garlic and onion until they are just collapsing.

2. Add mussels and stir briefly.

3. Add mustard, followed by beer, then put the lid on. Give the pot a jiggle.

4. Allow to boil over medium heat for about 7 minutes, until the shells of the mussels open. Discard those with unopened shells.

5. Stir in cream at this point if using. Toss parsley into the pot and stir.

6. Serve with a crusty baguette to mop up all the aromatic juices.

Note: Mussels should always be cleaned under cold running water, and the whiskers removed before cooking. Give the shells a good brush. I usually soak my mussels in cold water for at least 20 minutes to remove any excess dirt and salt.

This dish reminds me of my favourite weekend ritual whilst living in Switzerland. Almost every Sunday, I would jump on my bike and ride across the Swiss border into France. The marché that was an easy 10-kilometre bike ride away always left my pockets empty and my backpack full of groceries. My favourite seafood stall had everything I loved: fresh oysters, mountains of smoked salmon and of course, plump juicy mussels.

Episode 3

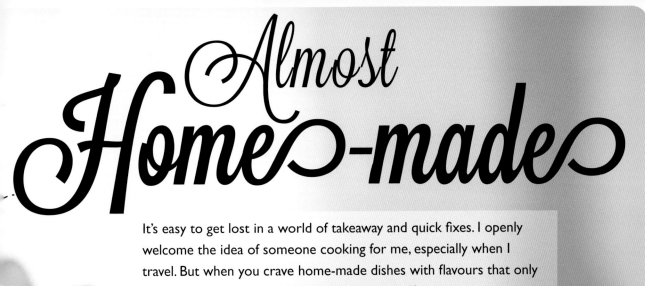

Almost Home-made

It's easy to get lost in a world of takeaway and quick fixes. I openly welcome the idea of someone cooking for me, especially when I travel. But when you crave home-made dishes with flavours that only you can create, nothing beats making it yourself.

In this section, store-bought alternatives can be used for some ingredients, and you can also make use of take-out food, which can spice up home-made meals. Perhaps for you, ordering these dishes at a neighbourhood café can be done at the push of a button. But give these recipes a try before you eat out the next time. The Crispy Phyllo is a must for your next small dinner party, and Home-made Lasagna will satisfy your craving for Italian food anytime.

Crunchy Spring Rolls with Fragrant Rice Noodles

Serves 2, makes 24 spring rolls

Spring Roll wrappers 18–24

Egg wash 1 egg, beaten

Cooking oil for deep-frying

Vietnamese rice noodles 160 g (5$^2/_3$ oz), cooked according to package instructions

Grilled chicken 140 g (5 oz), cut into pieces

Pickled carrots about 100 g (3$^1/_2$ oz)

Coriander a sprig

Bean sprouts a handful, blanched

Bird's eye chilli 1, finely sliced

Spring Roll Filling

Fresh prawns (shrimps) 80 g (2$^4/_5$ oz), peeled and deveined

Ground pork 220 g (7$^4/_5$ oz)

Shallots 2, peeled and finely chopped

Garlic 1 clove, peeled and crushed

Coriander 2 Tbsp

Water 1 Tbsp

Olive oil 1 Tbsp

Fish sauce 1 tsp

Ground white pepper a pinch

Sauce

Warm water 125 ml (4 fl oz / $^1/_2$ cup)

Sugar 3 Tbsp

Fish sauce 3 Tbsp + more if desired

Lime juice from 1–2 limes + more if desired

White vinegar 1 Tbsp

Garlic 2 cloves, peeled and minced

Bird's eye chilli 1

1. Prepare sauce. In a small jar, add water and sugar. Shake or stir until sugar has dissolved. Add the remaining sauce ingredients and mix. Add more fish sauce or lime juice if desired. Set sauce aside.

2. Prepare spring roll filling. In a food processor, blend prawns into a paste, then add pork and blend further. Add shallots, garlic, coriander, water and olive oil. Pulse for a few times until combined. Season with fish sauce and pepper. Pulse briefly to mix. Set aside.

3. Prepare spring rolls. Lay a spring roll wrapper in front, with the tip nearest to you such that it looks like a diamond shape. Lay another 3 sheets on top of the first one, leaving a 0.5-cm ($^1/_4$-in) border between each sheet.

4. Brush some egg wash onto the top corner. Place about 2 tsp filling in the middle of the wrapper. Bring in the two side corners, folding them over the filling. Fold the bottom corner up, over the filling. Roll until the top corner seals the spring roll. Brush more egg wash if needed to ensure spring roll is securely sealed. The wrapper should encase the filling firmly, but it shouldn't be too tight, since it will expand a little upon frying. Set aside on a clean dry tray, making sure there is a gap between each spring roll. Repeat until filling is used up, and cover with a moist kitchen towel.

5. Heat oil for deep-frying. When the temperature reaches 180°C (350°F), lower spring rolls into the oil. Deep-fry in batches for 3–5 minutes, making sure the fryer is not overcrowded. There should be enough room to flip the spring rolls. When spring rolls turn golden brown, remove from heat and drain off oil on a wire rack.

6. Place rice noodles on a large serving plate and arrange grilled chicken next to it. Garnish with pickled carrots, coriander, bean sprouts and bird's eye chilli. Serve with spring rolls and sauce.

The combination of mixed herbs and cool silky noodles with crunchy spring rolls is totally delicious. I like to make bite-size spring rolls, which are small compared to the giant cabbage-stuffed ones my mum makes. Crispy on the outside and juicy on the inside, these crunchy treats go really well with rice noodles. If you prefer, you can eat them on their own or wrapped up in crisp lettuce leaves.

Smoked Curry Fish Kedgeree

Serves 2–3

Basmati rice 175 g (6^1/$_4$ oz)

Large eggs 2

Onion 1, peeled and finely chopped

Butter 1 Tbsp

Red pepper (capsicum) ^{1}/$_2$, thinly sliced

Cardamom pod 1, crushed

Curry powder 1 tsp

Fish stock or water about 300 ml (10 fl oz / 1^1/$_4$ cup)

Smoked fish (e.g. haddock or cod) 250 g (9 oz), sliced or flaked

Coriander leaves a small bunch, shredded

1. Rinse rice under cold water until the water runs clear. Soak for 15–30 minutes, then drain and set aside.

2. Cook eggs in boiling water for about 6 minutes. Soak in cold water for 5 minutes, then peel and set aside.

3. Meanwhile, in a pan, sauté onion in butter. Keep stirring so that the butter gets a rich nutty flavour without burning the onions. Add red pepper, cardamom and curry powder. Cook for about 20 seconds, moving the spices around so they don't burn. When aromatic, add rice. Stir for about 2 minutes, until rice is well coated with spices.

4. Stir in fish stock or water. Add smoked fish, immersing the fish meat in the rice. Continue to add enough stock or water so that everything is immersed under 1 cm (½ in) of liquid. Put the lid on and reduce to low heat. Cook for 15–20 minutes, until the rice has absorbed all the liquid.

5. Using a fork, fluff up the rice and let it stand for 10 minutes with the lid on.

6. Stir in coriander and eggs. Serve immediately.

Smoked fish is one of my favourites. The smoky, salty taste is great with steamed rice or when flaked into an omelette. The spices in this recipe are flavourful but they don't overpower the fish — a classic combination.

Home-made Lasagna

Serves 4

Pasta sheets or lasagna noodles 450 g
  (1 lb), prepared according to package
  instructions

Parmesan cheese 160 g (5^2/$_3$ oz), grated

Bolognese Sauce

Cooking oil for frying

Onion 1, peeled and diced

Garlic 2 cloves, peeled and finely chopped

Carrot 1, peeled and diced

Celery 1 stalk, diced

Ground beef 300 g (10^1/$_2$ oz)

Ground pork 100 g (3^1/$_2$ oz)

Kidney beans 4 Tbsp

Oregano 1 tsp, chopped, or 1 tsp Italian herb mix

Nutmeg and cinnamon mix a sprinkle

Salt a pinch

Ground black pepper a pinch

Sugar 1 tsp

Tomato paste 2 Tbsp

Canned tomatoes 790 g (1 lb 12 oz)

Red wine 100 ml (3^1/$_3$ fl oz)

Water 500 ml (16 fl oz / 2 cups)

Creamy Sauce

Egg 1

Crème fraîche 400 ml (13^1/$_2$ fl oz)

Mascarpone cheese 95 g (3^1/$_3$ oz)

Salt to taste

Ground black pepper to taste

1. Preheat oven to 180°C (350°F).

2. Prepare Bolognese sauce. Heat oil in a large pan. Sauté onion, garlic, carrot and celery until onion slices turn translucent.

3. Push vegetables to the side of the pan and heat another 1 Tbsp oil. Add ground beef and pork. Break up large pieces with the back of the spatula.

4. Mix vegetables with meat. Cook just long enough for the meat to brown. Add kidney beans. Sprinkle oregano or herb mix, followed by nutmeg and cinnamon mix. Season with salt and pepper.

5. Combine sugar, tomato paste and canned tomatoes. Stir mixture into the meat and cook for 2 minutes more.

6. Pour in wine and allow it to reduce by about half. Add water and mix well. Bring to the boil and simmer for about 30 minutes to get a richer and thicker Bolognese sauce.

7. Meanwhile, prepare creamy sauce. Beat the egg and add to crème fraîche. Mix in Mascarpone cheese, then season with salt and pepper.

8. Assemble lasagna. Spoon some Bolognese sauce to cover the bottom of a baking tray. Arrange pasta sheet or lasagna noodles over the sauce. Spoon Bolognese sauce over the pasta. Continue layering until baking tray is sufficiently filled, with the pasta as the top layer. Pour creamy sauce over and top with generous sprinkles of cheese.

9. Bake for at least 45 minutes, until edges are crusty and brown.

10. Serve and indulge.

Lasagna is one of my all-time favourite comfort foods. A cheesy top and blankets of pasta in a rich tomato sauce satisfies even the most discerning eater. This recipe makes a decent amount of sauce, which can be frozen and thawed for other meals. I have taken a shortcut and made crème fraîche sauce instead of regular béchamel sauce. Creamy and smooth, this recipe will soon be a favourite of yours too.

Crispy Phyllo

Serves 2

Phyllo or puff pastry sheets about 12 layers, trimmed to required size

Melted butter for brushing pastry

Cod or Red Snapper fillets 2, about 0.5 cm ($^1/_4$ in) thick

Green peas 150 g ($5^1/_3$ oz)

Young asparagus spears 8, ends snapped off and halved

Egg wash 1 egg, beaten

Home-made Pesto Sauce

Basil leaves a generous handful

Garlic 2 cloves, peeled and chopped

Salt to taste

Ground black pepper to taste

Olive oil about 125 ml (4 fl oz / $^1/_2$ cup)

1. Preheat oven to 180°C (350°F).

2. Prepare pesto sauce. Place all ingredients for pesto sauce, except olive oil, in a food processor. Blend ingredients while drizzling in olive oil until you get a smooth and runny paste. Set aside until needed.

3. On a clean surface, brush one sheet of pastry with some melted butter. Place another sheet of pastry on top and brush butter over it. Repeat with a few more layers.

4. Halve a fish fillet and place one half of it on the buttered pastry sheets. Smear about 1 Tbsp pesto sauce onto the fish. Arrange peas and asparagus on top. Top with the other half of the fillet.

5. Brush egg wash onto the corners of the pastry sheets. Carefully roll up the pastry sheets to enclose the fish, forming a small parcel. If necessary, brush on more egg wash to seal the parcel more securely. Set aside on a greased baking tray.

6. Repeat steps 3–5 for remaining fish fillet and pastry sheets.

7. Bake pastry parcels in the oven for 20–25 minutes, until the pastry is golden and crispy. To test if the fish is done, insert a sharp knife down the centre of the pastry, where the fish would be. Touch the knife; if it is hot, the fish is cooked through.

8. Serve immediately.

Note: Phyllo pastry dries out quite quickly, so you have to work fast. Unused phyllo sheets should be placed under a moist towel to prevent it from drying out. And, if you are using cod fillets, make sure the pieces are not too thick so that it cooks thoroughly.

The French version of this dish is much more complex, with layers of crêpes and smoked fish wrapped together in a buttery package. My take on this dish is much easier and offers satisfying results too. The green peas add a taste of spring, making it perfect for an easy lunch as you sit and watch the world go by.

Devilled Eggs with Fried Oysters

Makes 12 servings

Eggs 6 + 1 for batter

Plain (all-purpose) flour 60 g (2 oz)

Ground black pepper $\frac{1}{4}$ tsp

Salt $\frac{1}{4}$ tsp

Cooking oil for deep-frying

Fresh oysters 12, shucked and drained

Dry breadcrumbs 50 g ($1\frac{2}{3}$ oz)

Avocado $\frac{1}{2}$, peeled, deseeded and mashed

Mayonnaise 2 Tbsp

Lemon juice from $\frac{1}{2}$ lemon

Small pickled onions 3, finely sliced

1. Beat 1 egg and set aside.

2. Combine flour with pepper and salt. Set aside.

3. In a deep saucepan, heat oil to deep-fry oysters.

4. When the oil is about 180°C (350°F), dip oysters in flour mixture, followed by beaten egg and finally the breadcrumbs, shaking off any excess batter. Drop coated oysters into the oil and deep-fry for about 1 minute, until the batter is crisp and golden. Drain on a wire rack.

5. Place remaining eggs in a saucepan of water and bring to the boil. Let eggs cook in boiling water for about 6–7 minutes, until the yolks are still moist in the middle but the whites are cooked.

6. Plunge eggs into cold water before peeling. Halve eggs and remove the yolks. Set the whites aside.

7. In a small bowl, mash egg yolks and add remaining ingredients, except pickled onions, to make a paste. Mash until it reaches a desired consistency. I like some chunks in mine. Spoon mixture back into the hollowed out eggs.

8. Top with oysters and pickled onions. Serve immediately.

To me, devilled eggs is a rather retro dish best left for 80s themed parties. However, after driving up the coast towards Rhode Island, I was inspired to give a new twist to an old classic. The combination of the fresh sea air and silky oysters enjoyed off the coast of Connecticut may have played a part in this recipe. I couldn't let this recipe go undiscovered amongst food lovers. This is an old-timer recipe with crunch and oomph — I love it! If you can't get hold of fresh oysters, mussels and anchovy fillets work well too.

Episode 4

In my opinion, fancy dining experiences are best enjoyed in a restaurant. Daily home-cooked meals should be quick and simple. I prefer to let my appetite and growling stomach dictate what pops up on my menu. I'm a lazy cook on weekdays, especially after a long day of shopping and eating out around the city. These recipes might be simple and far too easy for impressing guests, but they are definitely delicious servings that every home cook should have up their sleeves. Take five from dining out and chill with friends over these fuss-free treats, which can be prepared in a matter of minutes.

Take
Five

Crab Rice with Egg Ribbons

Serves 2

Cooking oil 1 Tbsp

Eggs 2, beaten with 1 tsp sugar

Fresh crab 1

Rice 200 g (7 oz), washed and rinsed

Rice wine vinegar 4 Tbsp, mixed with 1 tsp sugar

1. Heat 1 Tbsp oil in a pan. When oil is hot, add beaten eggs and make a rolled omelette by moving the pan away from you and back again in quick successive motions. If the omelette doesn't roll to the centre of the pan, use a spatula to do so. Leave to cool before cutting into thin strips. Set aside.

2. Rinse and clean the crab in cold water. Separate the legs and claws from the body. Lightly crack the shell on the crab pieces with a mallet, and remove visible gills. This will help to release the crab juices to flavour the rice. Arrange crab on top of rice in the rice cooker.

3. Add water for rice. If using a rice cooker, add water before placing crab on top. If cooking rice over the stove, make sure the water is about 0.5 cm (¼ in) above the rice before placing crab.

4. When rice is cooked, remove crab and let it cool for about 5 minutes before cracking the shell and scooping out the meat. Sprinkle crab meat over the rice and pour vinegar mixture over, fluffing a little with a fork before letting it sit for at least 5 minutes with the lid on.

5. Top with egg ribbons and leave to cool before serving.

Note: If using a pot or saucepan to cook rice, cover with a lid and cook on high heat for 1 minute, and then reduce to medium heat for 5 minutes before cooking over low heat for 10 minutes. When rice is done, turn off heat and place a cloth under the lid for 10 minutes to draw out excess moisture.

Fresh crab meat is definitely recommended. This dish is best served slightly warm and topped with satiny egg ribbons.

Crunchy Baked Tomatoes Over Orecchiette Pasta

Serves 2

Cherry tomatoes 250 g (9 oz), halved

Red pepper (capsicum) 1, sliced into wedges

Ground black pepper to taste

Anchovy fillets 4 or more if desired

Salt (optional) to taste

Dry breadcrumbs 70 g (2^1/$_2$ oz)

Extra virgin olive oil 2 Tbsp

Orecchiette pasta 225 g (8 oz)

Pecorino cheese 90 g (3^1/$_5$ oz), grated

Parsley a handful

1. Preheat oven to 180°C (350°F).

2. Place cherry tomatoes and red pepper in an oven-proof casserole dish. Season with pepper. Drape anchovy fillets over, using as many as you like. Season with salt if desired. Sprinkle breadcrumbs and drizzle a little olive oil on top.

3. Bake for about 15 minutes or until the tomatoes and peppers have slightly collapsed, and breadcrumbs are golden brown.

4. Meanwhile, prepare pasta according to package instructions, reserving about 2–3 Tbsp of its cooking liquid.

5. When pasta is cooked until al dente, quickly stir cheese into cooked pasta, mix in pasta cooking liquid at the same time if it is a little dry.

6. Stir in baked tomatoes and a handful of parsley.

Salty anchovies, sweet cherry tomatoes and a crunchy golden crust served with fresh pasta — a deliciously simple and different way to enjoy pasta outside of the normal carbonara and bolognese variety.

Crispy Arancini Balls

makes about 8 large Arancini balls

Cooking oil for deep-frying

Day-old risotto See risotto recipe on the right

Mozzarella cheese 55 g (2 oz), cubed

Plain (all-purpose) flour 200 g (7 oz)

Large eggs 2, beaten

Panko breadcrumbs 200 g (7 oz)

Sea salt (optional) to taste

Risotto

Butter 1 Tbsp

Onion 1, peeled and finely diced

Risotto rice 170 g (6 oz)

White wine 125 ml (4 fl oz / $^1/_2$ cup)

Hot chicken stock 500 ml (16 fl oz / 2 cups)

Parmesan Cheese 45 g (1$^1/_2$ oz)

1. Preheat oil in a deep-fryer or deep saucepan to 170°C (338°F).

2. Roll golf ball-sized portions of rice mixture with your hands.

3. Push a hole in the base of each ball. Fill each hole with a cube of Mozzarella cheese and roll to enclose the filling.

4. Roll the balls in flour, followed by beaten eggs, then panko breadcrumbs, shaking off any excess.

5. Deep-fry in batches, turning occasionally, until golden brown. This should take 3–4 minutes. Be careful as the oil may spit.

6. Drain on a wire rack, season with sea salt if desired and serve warm.

Risotto

1. To make risotto, heat butter in a deep saucepan. Sauté onion until translucent.

2. Add rice and stir-fry briefly. Stir in white wine.

3. Once wine has been absorbed, scoop some hot chicken stock over. Stir and let it simmer. Before the stock completely evaporates, ladle in more chicken stock. Stir and let it simmer. Repeat this for about 15 minutes, until rice is cooked but still firm.

4. Turn off heat and stir in Parmesan cheese.

5. Leave to cool before chilling it in the refrigerator.

Arancini is a very alluring Italian name for risotto balls. The best I have ever tasted was in Rome, in a tiny take-out cafe outside a train station. This recipe re-creates the delicious Italian flavour that brings me back to my time in Italy. Made up of plump rice encased in a crispy crust, bursting with rich cheesy flavours and a myriad of aromatic ingredients, these treats are simply delicious and addictive.

Pea Soup and Bagel Dumplings

Serves 2

Butter 30 g (1 oz)

Onion 1, peeled and finely chopped

Bacon 1 rasher

Potatoes 2, peeled and diced

Salt to taste

Ground Black Pepper to taste

Frozen or shelled peas 400 g (14 oz)

Vegetable stock or water 750 ml (24 fl oz / 3 cups)

Mint leaves a handful, chopped

Bagel Dumplings

Eggs 2

Milk 125 ml (4 fl oz / $1/2$ cup)

Salt to taste

Ground black pepper to taste

Four-day-old bagels 4, broken into small pieces

Marjoram and parsley mix 3 Tbsp, chopped

Dry breadcrumbs 75 g ($2^2/3$ oz)

Butter for pan-frying

Cooking oil for pan-frying

1. Melt butter in a heavy saucepan over medium heat. Add onion and bacon. Cook for about 5 minutes, until onion is translucent and soft, and the bacon crisp and browned.

2. Add potatoes and continue to cook for 5 minutes. Season with salt and pepper.

3. Add peas and stir for a minute before adding vegetable stock or water. Bring to a boil before reducing to a simmer, until everything is tender. This should take 10–15 minutes.

4. Add mint leaves before putting everything into a food processor.

5. Blend and serve with bagel dumplings.

Bagel Dumplings

1. Lightly beat eggs with milk. Whisk until combined. Season with salt and pepper.

2. Add bagels and marjoram-parsley mix, followed by breadcrumbs. Mix well and refrigerate for 15 minutes.

3. Using your hands, form golf ball-sized portions. Combine with some more breadcrumbs if it seems too wet.

4. Heat butter and a little oil in a pan. When oil is hot enough, pan-fry bagel dumplings until golden brown on all sides. Serve with pea soup.

This is a simple soup that can be created with frozen peas, and makes for a delicious light meal. The potatoes impart a nice texture and the smokiness of the bacon is a must in this hearty soup.

Nutty Baklava Parcels

Makes about 18 parcels

Mixed nuts (e.g. pistachios, walnuts, almonds) 300 g (10½ oz)

Sugar 2 Tbsp

Orange zest ½ tsp, grated

Melted butter for brushing

Phyllo or pastry sheets 225 g (8 oz), about 18 sheets

Syrup

Sugar 400 g (14 oz)

Water 250 ml (8 fl oz / 1 cup)

Orange rind from 1 orange

1. Lightly crush mixed nuts in a food processor. Tip crushed nuts into a bowl and mix with sugar and orange zest.

2. Preheat oven to 180°C (350°F).

3. Brush butter over a pastry sheet. Lay another pastry sheet on top and brush butter over the second sheet. Repeat until there are at least 6 layers. Add more layers if desired. Using a sharp knife, divide pastry stack into equal squares, each about twice the size of a mould in the muffin tray.

4. Push each square into a mould within a greased muffin tray. Top with mixed nuts. Bunch and fold down the wall of excess pastry sheets until they cover the mixed nuts and are level with the muffin mould. Brush butter over to securely seal the parcels.

5. Bake for 18–22 minutes, until the tops are nice and golden.

6. Meanwhile, combine all ingredients for syrup and bring to a boil. Simmer for about 15 minutes, until slightly thickened. Remove from heat.

7. When baklava parcels are ready, pour hot syrup over. Allow to cool before serving.

Gloriously sticky and crunchy, the nutty filling wrapped in a crispy parcel of buttery pastry is one of my favourites. I like to enjoy these treats with ice-cream and fairy floss for a girly afternoon session with friends. These are almost too perfect when paired with champagne!

Episode 5

The US cop a lot of flack for their notoriously unhealthy fast food habits. With all the hamburger joints, hotdog stands and hole-in-the-wall eateries, the US serves up some of the best fast food in the world. I get a little giddy at the amount of food you can get for just under 5 dollars — with loose change, juicy burgers with all the fixin's can fill a hungry tummy … amazing.

If you want to truly experience New York on a budget, grab a slice of thin-crust pizza in the East Village before parking yourself on a bench along the Upper West Side to savour it.

Gathering inspiration from some of the best fast food joints in Manhattan, Brooklyn and afar, I have re-created some take-out favourites which make New York a culinary hub for all budgets.

Take-out at home

Home-made Burgers

Makes 6 burgers

Ground beef 500 g (1 lb 1½ oz)
Small red onion 1, peeled and finely chopped
Worcestershire sauce a drizzle
Sea salt to taste
Ground black pepper to taste
Vacherin or Gruyère cheese 6 Tbsp, cubed
Olive oil for grilling
Burger buns 6, halved

Topping
Sunny-side-up eggs 6
Tomatoes 2, sliced
Lettuce leaves 6
Pickle slices a handful

Sauce
Pickles 45 g (1½ oz), finely chopped
Small pickled onions 4, finely chopped
Mayonnaise 3 Tbsp
Ketchup 1 tsp

1. Whisk all sauce ingredients together. Set aside.

2. Combine beef, onion and Worcestershire sauce. Season with salt and pepper.

3. Divide meat mixture into 6 portions and mould each portion into a patty.

4. For each patty, push some cheese into its centre. Encase the cheese and re-shape the patty.

5. Drizzle olive oil on a heated griddle. Cook patties for about 5 minutes on each side until they are slightly charred.

6. Smear sauce on burger buns and place patties on the bottom bun halves.

7. Arrange topping over patties. Cover with top bun halves and serve.

Mmmm ... the humble burger. Everyone should have a good recipe for this, and here is mine. A quick fix with oozing cheese stuffed in a succulent beef patty — delicious!

Yatai-style Yaki Udon

Serves 2

Udon 150 g (5$\frac{1}{3}$ oz)

Cooking oil for stir-frying

Eggs 2, beaten

Sliced pork 50 g (1$\frac{2}{3}$ oz)

Small cabbage $\frac{1}{4}$ head, roughly chopped

Oyster sauce 1 Tbsp

Light soy sauce 1 Tbsp

Mayonnaise (preferably Japanese) 1 Tbsp + more for garnishing

Spring onions (scallions) 2 stalks, cut into 5-cm (2-in) lengths

Red chilli 1, finely sliced

Sesame oil a drizzle

1. In a pot, bring udon to a boil for about 2 minutes. Drain and set aside.

2. Heat 1 Tbsp oil in a large pan. Lightly stir-fry eggs for about 1 minute, until nice and fluffy. Remove from heat and set aside.

3. Add a little more oil to the pan and stir-fry pork, moving it side to side until the meat changes colour.

4. Add extra oil if needed and cook cabbage for about 5 minutes, until it softens but still has some crunch.

5. Add udon. Continue to stir-fry, moving the noodles around so that they don't stick to the pan.

6. Add oyster sauce, soy sauce and 1 Tbsp mayonnaise. Continue to toss until well mixed.

7. Add cooked egg, three-quarters of the spring onions and red chilli. Drizzle sesame oil. Toss a few more times and scoop onto serving dishes. Top with mayonnaise for a real Yatai experience.

8. Garnish with remaining spring onions and serve.

Japan's answer to a food truck is a *Yatai*, an oversized wheelbarrow that is pulled to various corners of the city selling home-style favourites. Quick, easy and totally delicious, this Japanese fast food is one of my favourites for a quick dinner. There are no rules when it comes to stir-fried noodles. Almost any ingredient can be used. Cabbage is a traditional favourite since it is sweet and crunchy. Eggs are also perfect additions. I like to use udon for this dish, but you may substitute it with other types of noodles.

Crispy Open Dumplings

Makes 18–20 dumplings

Gyoza pastry 18–20 pieces

Cooking oil for frying

White sesame seeds a sprinkle, toasted

Garlic 4 cloves, peeled and roughly chopped

Bird's eye chillies At least 2, finely sliced

Ground pork 200 g (7 oz)

Fish sauce a drizzle, or a sprinkle of salt and ground white pepper

Mix of basil and mint leaves 2 handfuls, roughly chopped

Small cabbage 1/4 head, finely shredded

1. Drop gyoza pastry into hot oil and fry until lightly golden. This should take about 20 seconds on each side. Sprinkle some sesame seeds and drain off excess oil on a wire rack.

2. In a separate pan, heat about 1 Tbsp oil. Fry garlic and chillies until aromatic. Add pork and continue to stir-fry for a minute, until meat is cooked through and the colour has changed. Season with fish sauce or a sprinkle of salt and pepper. Remove from heat, then stir in basil and mint leaves.

3. Arrange shredded cabbage on fried gyoza pastry. Top with a generous amount of pork mix and serve.

Note: For a less spicy version, halve chillies and remove seeds with a knife before slicing them.

In Orange County, Los Angeles, my grandpa owns a Chinese restaurant that makes the best dumplings. My family are very picky when it comes to Chinese food, especially dumplings — even the dough is made from scratch. Wanting to be a little silly one day, I tried to take a shortcut to a family recipe by using store-bought pastry. Having a difficult time trying to wrap my dumplings, I gave up and decided to make something totally different and came up with this recipe of fresh herbs and meat on a crispy pastry.

Beer-battered Fish 'n' Chips

Serves 2

Plain (all-purpose) flour 200 g (7 oz)

Canola oil for deep-frying

Baking powder 2 tsp

Salt a pinch

Chilled beer or sparkling water 225 ml (7²/₃ fl oz)

Haddock or cod fillets 2, about 200 g (7 oz) each

Garlic Fries

Large potatoes 3, washed and peeled

Canola oil for deep-frying

Garlic 3 cloves, peeled and minced

Parsley 1 Tbsp, finely chopped

Salt a sprinkle

1. Chill flour in the freezer for 15 minutes before use.

2. Heat oil in a deep-fryer to 185°C (365°F).

3. Quickly whisk baking powder and chilled flour along with salt and beer, until you get a thick batter.

4. Coat fish fillets with batter and deep-fry one at a time, until crisp and golden.
   Ensure that the temperature stays at 185°C (365°F) before frying the second fillet.

5. Drain fish fillets of oil on a wire rack.

6. Serve with garlic fries and garlic-infused mayonnaise or aioli.

Garlic Fries

1. Cut potatoes into 0.5-cm (¹/₄-in) strips. Wash well under cold water before draining.

2. Parboil potatoes until just soft but not falling apart. Drain well and chill in the refrigerator for 1 hour.

3. Heat oil in a deep fryer to 120°C (250°F).

4. Fry potato strips until golden. Leave to cool before chilling in the refrigerator for another hour.

5. Heat oil to 180°C (350°F).

6. Mix chips with garlic and parsley.

7. Fry chips until it is crispy and golden. Season with salt and serve alongside fish fillets.

Note: The beer must be very cold to achieve a tempura-like batter.

If you prefer, you can bake your chips instead. Drizzle oil over potato strips before baking them at 230°C (450°F) for 30 minutes, until golden brown and crispy. Toss with garlic and parsley, then serve with fish fillets.

Fish 'n' Chips may be a British classic, but if you travel north of New York towards Connecticut and Maine you'll find a big following of seafood lovers waiting for the fresh catch of the day. Crispy batter, almost like that of Japanese tempura, and garlic chips, are perfect with a cold beer by the sea.

Easy Peasy Cheesy Cabonara

Serves 2

Rigatoni or any other pasta 250 (9 oz)

Spicy Italian sausage 1

Cooking oil 1 Tbsp

Broccoli 150 g (5^{1}/$_{3}$ oz)

Fresh eggs 2

Parmesan cheese 50 g (^{4}/$_{5}$ oz), grated + more if desired

Single (light) cream or full-cream milk 125 ml (4 fl oz / ^{1}/$_{2}$ cup)

Salt a generous sprinkle

Ground black pepper to taste

1. Cook pasta according to package instructions.

2. Remove sausage casing. Heat oil in a pan and fry sausage, breaking it into little pieces with the back of the spatula. Add broccoli and continue to fry until the meat is completely cooked through. Remove from heat and set aside.

3. Crack eggs into a bowl. Mix in cheese, cream or milk, and a sprinkle of salt and pepper.

4. When pasta is cooked until al dente, drain and reserve about 125 ml (4 fl oz / ^{1}/$_{2}$ cup) of its cooking liquid.

5. Immediately add hot pasta into the egg and milk mixture. Combine thoroughly. Mix in some of the pasta's cooking liquid if it is too dry.

6. Stir in sausage and broccoli. Sprinkle more cheese if desired. Serve immediately.

If you ever find yourself in Rome, be sure to seat yourself in an Italian café surrounded by locals and order the Pasta Alla Carbonara. Deliciously rich and creamy, this is a simple yet satisfying meal that looks like the Italian flag in a bowl. My version is a typical Italian recipe borrowed from friends, with my own additions of broccoli and a spicy Italian sausage.

Episode 6

Trying out new recipes can always be a little daunting even for an experienced cook. The recipes and tips in this section are gathered from the talented and creative chefs I met during my travels. These ideas are fantastic for a quiet night at home or even for entertaining guests. What I love about them is that they are big on flavour yet simple to prepare. Sweet and sour, crunchy and soft, spicy and cool … your taste buds will go wild!

Creative
Food

Creamy Salmon Pot Pies

Makes 4 pies

Cooking oil 1 Tbsp

Onion 1, peeled and chopped

Garlic 2 cloves, peeled and finely chopped

Carrot 1, peeled and chopped

Milk or single (light) cream 250 ml (8 fl oz / 1 cup)

Fish stock 250 ml (8 fl oz / 1 cup)

Salmon fillets 2, each 200 g (7 oz), sliced into bite sized pieces

Whole grain mustard 1 tsp

Corn kernels 85 g (3 oz)

Spinach 2 handfuls, washed and roughly chopped

Parsley a handful, roughly chopped

Boiled egg 1, peeled and quartered

Puff pastry 2–4 sheets

Egg wash 1 egg, beaten

1. Preheat oven to 180°C (350°F).

2. Heat oil in a saucepan. Lightly sauté onion and garlic until onion is translucent. Add carrot and continue to cook for about 1 minute.

3. Add milk and fish stock. Bring to the boil, then lightly place fish slices into the pan. Bring to the boil again before reducing immediately to a simmer.

4. Stir in whole grain mustard. Add corn and spinach, followed by parsley.

5. Pour mixture into individual ramekins. Divide egg quarters among ramekins and cover with a sheet of puff pastry. Make sure the pastry does not touch the liquid, rather, it should sit on the rim of the ramekin, or it won't rise.

6. Brush with egg wash and bake in the oven for at least 20 minutes, until the puff is nice and golden brown.

7. Serve immediately.

Note: Depending on the size of your serving bowl or ramekin, the number of pastry sheets you need varies. If the pastry sheets are large, you can trim them to fit over the lid of each ramekin.

Mustard gives a rich, flavourful sauce that matches well with spinach and salmon. Topped with golden puff pastry, this is a delicious comfort food.

Roasted Pumpkin Soup with Fresh Mango

Serves 4

Pumpkin 500 g (1 lb 1$^1/_2$ oz), peeled and de-seeded

Garlic 5 cloves, ends chopped and unpeeled

Onions 2, ends chopped and halved, unpeeled

Olive oil a drizzle

Salt to taste

Ground black pepper to taste

Vegetable stock 500 ml (16 fl oz / 2 cups)

Nutmeg and cinnamon mix a sprinkle

Mango 1, peeled and cubed

1. Preheat oven to 180°C (350°F).

2. Line a roasting tray with foil. Arrange pumpkin, garlic and onions onto the tray.

3. Drizzle olive oil and sprinkle salt and pepper.

4. Roast in the oven for about 35 minutes, until everything is slightly burnt at the edges and tender.

5. Place pumpkin in a deep saucepan. Peel garlic and onion, and add to the saucepan as well.

6. Add stock and bring to the boil, then reduce to a simmer. Sprinkle nutmeg and cinnamon mix. Simmer for another 15–20 minutes.

7. Leave to cool, then blend in a food processor until it reaches a desired consistency.

8. Ladle into serving bowls. Garnish with fresh mango cubes and serve.

When I was travelling in Europe, I was very lucky to have met a lot of talented and innovative chefs. This one is inspired by a wine bar in Eastern Europe. Mango sweetens a classic recipe in more ways than one.

Crunchy Croqueta and Arugula Salad

Makes about 24 croqueta

Corn kernels 200 g (7 oz), fresh or defrosted

Butter 40 g (1^1/$_3$ oz)

Plain (all-purpose) flour 5 Tbsp

Milk 250 ml (8 fl oz / 1 cup)

Ham 25 g (^{4}/$_5$ oz), finely sliced

Parmesan cheese 25 g (^{4}/$_5$ oz)

Cooking oil for frying

Coating

Plain (all-purpose) flour a handful

Eggs 2, beaten

Dry breadcrumbs 75–100 g (2^2/$_3$–3^1/$_2$ oz)

Salad

Arugula 2 handfuls

Cherry tomatoes a small handful, halved

Red onion 1, peeled and finely sliced

Cooked white beans 200 g (7 oz), drained

Vinaigrette

Red vinegar 30 ml (1 fl oz)

Orange juice 1 Tbsp

Dijon mustard ^{1}/$_2$ tsp

Extra virgin olive oil 4 Tbsp

Salt a sprinkle

Ground black pepper a sprinkle

1. Mix all ingredients for vinaigrette, except salt and pepper, until well combined. Sprinkle in salt and pepper and set aside.

2. If using frozen corn kernels, defrost before pulsing them in a food processor until they have broken up but are not completely puréed. Melt butter in a heavy saucepan. Add flour and whisk until it comes together. Keep the mixture moving so it doesn't burn.

3. Slowly pour in half of the milk and whisk to combine. Continue to stir for another 2 minutes after all the milk and flour come together.

4. Add remaining milk and continue to stir until a thick creamy sauce forms. Continue to whisk over low heat to cook off the flour, until the creamy mixture almost pulls away from the pan.

5. Squeeze out water from the corn and add to the cream mixture. Add ham and Parmesan cheese at this point. Cover and refrigerate for at least 3 hours, preferably overnight, until corn paste is firm.

6. Spoon out portions of corn paste and mould each one into a round croqueta. Prepare coating ingredients. Coat each croqueta with flour, followed by beaten eggs and finally breadcrumbs.

7. Heat oil in a deep saucepan for frying. When oil is sufficiently hot, lightly drop in croquetas and fry until golden brown. This should take about 45 seconds.

8. Set croquetas aside on a wire rack to drain excess oil.

9. Mix salad ingredients in a large bowl. Mix in vinaigrette and toss lightly.

10. Serve salad with crunchy croquetas.

I can't imagine anything better than crispy pockets of silky béchamel-filled balls. These croquetas (or croquettes) are great for parties. Eat them by the handful or with a refreshing salad of cherry tomatoes, arugula and red onion.

Cheesy Potato and Spinach Bake

Serves 3–4

Ricotta cheese 170 g (6 oz)

Feta cheese 45 g (1¹/₂ oz), roughly crumbled

Milk 2 Tbsp

Salt a sprinkle

Ground black pepper a sprinkle

Baby spinach leaves 110 g (4 oz), washed and drained

Lemon zest from 1 lemon

Large potatoes 3, peeled and sliced

Butter for greasing

Mozzarella cheese 45 g (1¹/₂ oz), grated

1. Combine 140 g (5 oz) Ricotta cheese, Feta cheese and milk in a bowl. Sprinkle salt and pepper if desired.

2. Finely chop spinach and add to the Ricotta cheese mix. Combine until just mixed. Add lemon zest.

3. Preheat oven to 180°C (350°F).

4. Boil water in a pot to cook sliced potatoes until just tender. Drain and set aside.

5. Grease a casserole dish with butter. Cover the bottom with a layer of potatoes and spread Ricotta-spinach mix over it. Continue to alternate the layers in this manner, ending with potatoes on the topmost layer.

6. Spread remaining Ricotta cheese over the topmost layer of potatoes. Sprinkle Mozzarella cheese over.

7. Bake for at least 35 minutes, until everything is cooked through and golden brown on top.

8. Serve warm.

This recipe brings together a handful of simple ingredients that make a flavourful dish. Salty Feta cheese and the creaminess of Ricotta go delightfully well with floury potatoes.

Crab Cakes with Spinach and Poached Eggs

Makes 4 crab cakes

Large potatoes 2, peeled and chopped

Hard-boiled eggs 2, peeled and diced

Onion 1, peeled and finely chopped

Coriander 2 Tbsp, finely chopped

Crab meat 300 g (10 1/2 oz), shredded

Dry breadcrumbs 70–110 g (2 1/2–4 oz), mixed with white sesame seeds

Olive oil 3 Tbsp

Eggs 4, for poaching

Garlic 2 cloves, peeled and finely chopped

Spinach 2 handfuls, washed and drained

Butter 1 Tbsp

Coating

Plain (all-purpose) flour 5 Tbsp, for frying / dredging

Egg 1, lightly beaten

Fresh breadcrumbs 50 g (1 2/3 oz)

Sweet Chilli Sauce

Red chillies 5, finely chopped

Garlic 3 cloves, peeled and finely chopped

Sugar 3 Tbsp

Fish sauce 1/2 tsp

1. Place all ingredients for sweet chilli sauce in a saucepan. Add a splash of water and bring to the boil. Simmer until slightly thickened. Set aside to cool.

2. In a pot, bring water and potatoes to the boil. Reduce to a steady simmer and cook until potatoes are tender. This should take 12–15 minutes. Drain well and immediately mash, leaving some chunks of potato. Set aside to cool.

3. Lightly mix diced eggs, onion and coriander into mashed potatoes.

4. Stir in crab meat. Add three-quarters of the dry breadcrumb mix to bring it all together. Add more breadcrumbs if needed. Form 4 patties with mixture.

5. Prepare coating for patties. Lightly coat patties with flour, followed by egg and then fresh breadcrumbs. Removing excess as you go through the dredging process.

6. Heat oil in a shallow frying pan and lightly cook patties until golden brown on each side. Set aside to drain off oil.

7. Poach eggs.

8. Meanwhile, fry garlic and spinach in butter. Remove from heat when spinach has wilted.

9. Arrange spinach on serving plates. Top with crab patties and poached eggs. Drizzle sweet chilli sauce over and serve.

Note: If you want to give the crab cakes a creamier texture, add 2 Tbsp sour cream to mashed potatoes in step 3.

Forget the typical eggs on toast and try crab cakes with perfectly poached eggs for a change. Here's my rendition of this wonderful recipe that can brighten up any morning.

Episode 7

I have a major sweet tooth. Whether it's a decadent chocolate ganache cake or a simple cheesecake with jewels of toffee, a perfect meal is complete only if I end it off with something sweet. New York is the perfect destination for satisfying sweet cravings. Although baking may require a little precision and attention, I have collected a few of my favourite recipes that are almost foolproof for the novice baker. If you feel like adding an extra square of chocolate, you are strongly encouraged to do so!

Sweet Treats

Almost New York Cheesecake

Makes one 22-cm (9-in) round cake

Cream cheese 750 g (1 lb 10¹/₂ oz)

Sugar 200 g (7 oz)

Eggs 3

Mascarpone cheese 225 g (8 oz)

Lemon zest from 1 lemon

Vanilla extract 1 tsp

Crust

Sweet Biscuits 200 g (7 oz)

Almonds 2 Tbsp

Butter 6 Tbsp, melted

Caramel Shards

Castor sugar 225 g (8 oz)

Water 2 Tbsp

1. Place a small tray of water on the lowest rack in the oven. Preheat oven to 230°C (450°F).

2. Prepare crust. Blend biscuits and almonds in a food processor until they are crushed and resemble a sandy texture. Alternatively, pound with a mallet. Add half the butter and mix until you get a wet sandy consistency. Add remaining butter and mix until it comes together when you squeeze it between your hands. Press the crumbs firmly onto the bottom of a greased cake pan, or all around the springform pan. Refrigerate until needed.

3. Prepare filling. In a bowl, beat cream cheese and sugar until smooth and well combined. Add the eggs one at a time, beating to mix well after each addition. Add Mascarpone cheese, lemon zest and vanilla extract. Scrap the sides of the bowl and continue to mix until just combined and smooth.

4. Pour filling into prepared crust and smooth the top with the back of a spatula.

5. Place cheesecake on the rack above the water bath and bake for 15 minutes.

6. Reduce the temperature to 150°C (300°F) and continue to bake for another 30 minutes, until the cheesecake jiggles when moved.

7. Leave to cool at room temperature before refrigerating.

8. While waiting for cheesecake to chill, simmer ingredients for caramel shards over low heat until it turns a nice amber-gold colour. Drizzle hot liquid caramel onto a lined baking tray. Leave to cool until it hardens into crunchy caramel shards.

9. Break caramel shards into pieces and use them to garnish cheesecake before serving.

Note: Depending on the weather, the caramel shards may melt if left at room temperature, so prepare them only when ready to serve.

My dad loves cheesecake, so I'm adamant to put in a recipe that pays homage to his sweet tooth. New York has a love affair with two types of cheesecake, either Jewish or Italian. I've combined the two to produce a cheesecake with a Jewish-style texture and an Italian ingredient — Mascarpone cheese. If using a springform cake pan, be sure to line the crust all the way to the top.

Orange Coconut Syrup Cake

Makes about 6 mini loaves

Butter 125 g (4$^1/_2$ oz) + more for greasing

Castor sugar 175 g (6$^1/_4$ oz)

Orange rind from 1 orange

Eggs 2

Desiccated coconut 50 g (1$^2/_3$ oz)

Self-raising flour 185 g (6$^2/_3$ oz), sifted

Milk 125 ml (4 fl oz / $^1/_2$ cup)

Syrup

Sugar 220 g (7$^4/_5$ oz)

Water 180 ml (6 fl oz / $^3/_4$ cup)

Orange juice 2 Tbsp

1. Preheat oven to 175°C (347°F).

2. Beat butter, castor sugar and orange rind until creamy and light.

3. Add eggs one at a time, beating to mix well after each addition.

4. Stir in coconut with a wooden spoon until well mixed. Add flour and milk in batches, alternating their additions. Stir until just combined.

5. Pour into greased loaf pans and bake for 12–15 minutes, until the top is golden brown.

6. Boil syrup ingredients in a small saucepan over medium heat until sugar has dissolved. Simmer for 5 minutes until syrup is thick.

7. Pour syrup over warm cake and serve.

Note: Each mini loaf pan is about 11 x 6 x 6-cm (4$^1/_2$ x 2$^1/_2$ x 2$^1/_2$-in). You can also bake this in a regular 23 x 13 x 8-cm (9 x 5 x 3-in) loaf pan, but increase baking time by about 20–25 minutes.

I love using citrus fruits in my desserts. I have made many variations of this cake, and the combination of coconut and orange is one of my favourites. I like to use a lot of orange rind to give a tart and zesty flavour, which goes perfectly with a cup of tea. This special treat can lift up your spirits even on a dreary day.

Sweet Caramel Cake

Makes one 18-cm (7-in) bundt cake

Butter for greasing

Self raising flour 150 g (5$^1/_3$ oz) + more for dusting, sifted

Eggs 4

Condensed milk 1 can, about 375 ml (12 fl oz / 1$^1/_2$ cups)

Banana 1, peeled and sliced

Caramel Sauce

Cold butter 3 Tbsp, cubed

Brown sugar 200 g (7 oz)

Single (light) cream 125 ml (4 fl oz / $^1/_2$ cup)

Vanilla seeds from 1 pod

1. Preheat oven to 180°C (350°F).

2. Brush a bundt pan with butter, then dust with flour. Shake off excess flour.

3. Place flour in a mixing bowl. Make a well in the centre of the flour. Crack eggs and pour condensed milk into the well. Whisk everything together until well combined. Note that the more you mix, the denser the cake will be. I like a denser cake, but if you want something lighter, stop mixing once everything is well combined.

4. Pour into bundt pan and bake for about 35 minutes, until the top has browned.

5. Meanwhile, prepare caramel sauce. Whisk 2 Tbsp cubed butter, brown sugar and cream together over low heat. Continue to whisk until all the sugar dissolves, or it will be grainy. When mixture thickens, remove from heat and add vanilla seeds. Add remaining cold butter cubes to give the sauce a nice sheen.

6. Serve cake with banana and caramel sauce.

There are a lot of great spots for coffee and cake in New York. Making a decision can be difficult whether you are choosing a simple cake from a local bakery or ordering a bespoke designer cake. To make my life easier, I usually bake my own cakes. A small kitchen definitely doesn't allow much space for a giant stand mixer, so I tend to stick to easy cakes that require less effort and cleaning up. This Portuguese-inspired dessert is great with bananas and a rich caramel sauce.

Nutty Sticky Scrolls

Makes 12–15 scrolls

Yeast 7 g (¹/₅ oz)

Sugar 2 Tbsp

Warm milk 375 ml (12 fl oz / 1¹/₂ cups)

Plain (all-purpose) flour 500 g (1 lb 1¹/₂ oz) + more if needed

Salt a pinch

Egg 1

Butter 50 g (1²/₃ oz), melted + more for greasing

Castor sugar 50 g (1²/₃ oz)

Brown sugar 50 g (1²/₃ oz)

Ground cinnamon 1 tsp

Topping

Pecans and almonds 110 g (4 oz), roughly chopped

Butter 4 Tbsp

Ground cinnamon ¹/₂ tsp

Brown sugar 200 g (7 oz)

1. Dissolve yeast and sugar in warm milk. Let it stand for about 10 minutes until it gets frothy.

2. Mix flour and salt in a large bowl. Make a well in the centre of the mixture. Pour frothy yeast mixture and egg into the well. Bring everything together to form a dough. Knead for about 5 minutes, until everything comes together and the dough separates from the bowl. Add more flour if necessary. Cover the bowl with a towel and place in a warm area for 1 hour.

3. Preheat oven to 180°C (350°F).

4. Punch dough down on a work surface dusted with flour. Knead dough a little to bring it back into shape. Roll out dough without over stretching it, until it is about 17.5 x 15 cm (7 x 6 in).

5. Dot butter all over the dough, then sprinkle sugars and cinnamon all over. Start from the bottom and roll up loosely. Cut roll into 4-cm (1¹/₂-in) lengths.

6. Meanwhile, prepare topping. Lightly toast nuts in a pan. Combine toasted nuts with the rest of the topping ingredients and mix well. Smear onto a baking tray and arrange dough pieces on top, leaving a 5-cm (2-in) gap between each piece of dough. Leave to rise for 45 minutes to 1 hour, until dough pieces have doubled in size.

7. Bake until the buns have risen and are golden. This should take 20–25 minutes.

8. Invert the buns onto a serving plate. Garnish with extra syrup from the bottom of the pan and serve.

This recipe was inspired by a buffet of ideas that started as early as making Chelsea buns during my Home Economic classes at high school to sampling cinnamon buns in Sweden. The combination of nuts, cinnamon and sugar is fantastic and truly addictive to the last bite.

Chocolate Cake with Toasted Marshmallows

Makes two 20-cm (8-in) cakes

Plain (all-purpose) flour 225 g (8 oz) + more for dusting

Sugar 300 g (10½ oz)

Cocoa powder 85 g (3 oz)

Bicarbonate of soda 1 tsp

Baking powder 1 tsp

Salt a pinch

Milk 125 ml (4 fl oz / ½ cup)

Sour cream 125 ml (4 fl oz / ½ cup)

Butter 150 g (5⅓ oz), melted + more for greasing

Large eggs 2

Vanilla seeds from 1 pod

Brewed coffee 250 ml (8 fl oz / 1 cup), cooled

Glacé or Maraschino cherries 70 g (2½ oz), drained and chopped

Cherry Jam for topping

Marshmallows for topping

Chocolate Ganache for topping

Crushed nuts for topping

Chocolate Ganache

Dark chocolate 200 g (7 oz), chopped

Single (light) cream 125 ml (4 fl oz / ½ cup)

1. Preheat oven to 180°C (350°F).

2. Sift flour, sugar, cocoa powder, bicarbonate of soda, baking powder and salt at least three times. Place mixture into an electric mixer.

3. Combine milk, sour cream, butter, eggs and vanilla seeds in another bowl. Whisk until wet ingredients are well mixed.

4. With the mixer beating on low speed, add wet ingredients to the dry ones. Add coffee and cherries. Continue to beat until evenly mixed.

5. Grease cake pan with butter and dust with some flour. Pour batter into cake pan and bake for 35–40 minutes. Test doneness by inserting a skewer into the centre of the cake. It should come out clean if cake is done.

6. Meanwhile, prepare chocolate ganache. Melt chocolate in a bain marie or microwave oven. When chocolate turns soft, pour cream over and let it stand for 3 minutes before mixing.

7. Spread cherry jam on top of the cake and arrange marshmallows all over. Use a blow torch to toast the marshmallows. Alternatively, toast marshmallows over an open flame before arranging onto cake.

8. Drizzle chocolate ganache and top off with generous sprinkles of crushed nuts before serving.

A creation inspired by an Australian favourite — the Rocky Road. This is really easy to prepare and so enjoyable to eat. Get ready for decadent indulgence with nuts, marshmallows, chocolate and glacé cherries all rolled into one.

Episode 8

Living in France met all my expecations. Paris is absolutely worth visiting for its culture, lifestyle and of course food. For those travelling on a budget, bistros and even upscale restaurants offer great lunches that allow diners to sample the menu. I've collected a bunch of recipes that I borrowed from friends, and I hope they will bring a bit of the chic Parisian lifestyle that I experienced to your home. Bon Appetit!

Paris in
New York

Yellowtail Tartare

Serves 2

Sashimi-grade yellowtail 350 g (12$\frac{1}{2}$ oz), diced
Cherry tomatoes 5, finely chopped
Avocado $\frac{1}{2}$, peeled, deseeded and cubed
Caviar pearls for garnishing

Dressing
Crème fraîche 1 Tbsp
Shallot 1, peeled and finely diced
Capers 1 tsp, finely chopped
Tarragon 1 tsp, finely shredded
Pickled cucumber 1 Tbsp, finely chopped
Lime juice from 1 lime
Sea salt a pinch
Ground black pepper a pinch
Olive oil to taste

1. Place yellowtail, cherry tomatoes and avocado in a mixing bowl. Set aside.
2. In a separate bowl, combine dressing ingredients. Drizzle enough olive oil to get a loose dressing.
3. Lightly mix dressing into yellowtail mixture. Be careful not to break the fish.
4. Garnish with caviar pearls.
5. Serve chilled.

I prefer the less overpowering flavours of yellowtail. However, raw tuna or salmon is great too when served with chunky potato wedges and a crispy green salad. When working with raw fish, always ensure the fish is of sashimi grade. Keep tartare in the fridge over a bowl of ice to make sure it stays super fresh.

Braised Chicken with Cheesy Toast

Serves 2–3

Olive oil for frying

Chicken thigh 4–6 pieces

Butter 2 Tbsp

Garlic 2 cloves, peeled and chopped

Onions 4, peeled and sliced

Bay leaf 1

Salt a sprinkle

Ground black pepper a sprinkle

Thyme 2 sprigs

Treacle or brown sugar 1 tsp

Worcestershire sauce 1 tsp

Red wine (optional) 250 ml (8 fl oz / 1 cup)

Vegetable stock 500 ml (16 fl oz / 2 cups)

Gruyère cheese 225 g (8 oz), grated

Baguette 1, sliced

1. Heat olive oil in a pan. Cook chicken pieces until they have browned but are not yet cooked on the insides. Set aside.

2. Melt butter over medium heat. Fry garlic, onions, bay leaf, salt and pepper. When onions are slightly brown, add thyme, followed by treacle (or brown sugar) and Worcestershire sauce.

3. Pour in the wine if using and let it reduce to about half before adding in stock. Add browned chicken and cover with a lid. Simmer for about 25 minutes, until chicken is cooked through.

4. Meanwhile, sprinkle cheese over baguette slices and toast until cheese has melted.

5. Enjoy stew with cheesy toast.

One of my favourite cooking techniques is braising. This is a quick braise using the flavours of sweet onions and chicken, perfect for colder days. The crusty cheese-covered baguette is delicious when dunked into the stew. I've included red wine to give it a bit more body, but feel free to leave it out.

Raspberry Custard Tarts

Makes about 20 mini tarts

Store-bought pastry 20 small sheets

Plain (all-purpose) flour for dusting

Butter for greasing

Egg white for brushing

Custard

Milk 500 ml (16 fl oz / 2 cups)

Vanilla pod 1, seeds scraped and pod reserved

Egg yolks 3

Sugar 110 g (4 oz)

Corn flour (cornstarch) or plain (all-purpose) flour 40 g (1^1/$_3$ oz), sifted

Raspberries 170 g (6 oz)

1. Preheat oven to 180°C (350°F).

2. Roll out pastry on a floured surface, until it is about 3 mm thick. Using a floured cookie cutter, cut out dough rounds such that they fit nicely into the moulds in the tart pan.

3. Press gently to fit the dough rounds in a greased tart pan. Remove any excess dough. Refrigerate for 30 minutes to prevent the pastry from shrinking upon baking.

4. Prick dough all over with a fork and bake for about 7 minutes, until the pastry is a golden colour.

5. Remove from oven and brush pastry with a little egg white to prevent the pastry from becoming sticky or soggy.

6. Return to the oven and bake for 8–10 minutes more to get a golden finish.

7. Set aside to cool.

Custard

1. Heat milk with vanilla pod and seeds until just heated through. Remove from heat and discard vanilla pod.

2. In a separate bowl, beat egg yolks with sugar until mixture becomes pale.

3. Whisk flour into eggs, then slowly pour in milk while whisking. Once ^{1}/$_4$ of the milk has been added, you can do so more quickly. Whisking continuously, heat mixture over low to medium heat until it thickens. Cook for another 5 minutes to remove any floury taste.

4. Pour into a baking tray lined with cling film. Cover with another sheet of cling film to prevent formation of a skin. Leave aside to cool.

5. When custard has cooled, spoon into cooled crusts and top with raspberries before serving.

Note: You can substitute raspberries with other fruits of your choice.

Making your own pastry can be daunting and time consuming in a tiny kitchen with little work space. To save all the trouble, you can use good-quality ready-made dough from the bakery. The buttery pastry is topped with a sweet custard of fresh milk and vanilla — absolutely divine.

Choux Crème with Chocolate Ganache

Makes about 20 choux puffs

Whipped Cream 170 ml (5³/₄ fl oz)

Choux Puffs

Water 250 ml (8 fl oz / 1 cup)

Butter 100 g (3¹/₂ oz)

Sugar 1 Tbsp

Salt a pinch

Plain (all-purpose) flour 125 g (4¹/₂ oz), sifted

Eggs 4

Chocolate Ganache

Pure thickened cream 125 g (4¹/₂ oz)

Dark chocolate 125 g (4¹/₂ oz), broken into small chunks

Unsalted butter 10 g (¹/₃ oz)

1. Preheat oven to 220°C (425°F).

2. Prepare choux puffs. In a saucepan, bring water, butter, sugar and salt to the boil. Remove from heat and add flour. Beat vigorously with a wooden spoon. Return to heat and work mixture until it detaches from the saucepan.

3. Remove from heat and beat eggs in one at a time, making sure one egg is well mixed into the batter before adding the next one. Continue to beat vigorously until the finished dough is soft, sticky and well combined.

4. On a baking tray lined with greaseproof paper, spoon or pipe dollops of batter. Each dollop should be about 2 tsp worth of batter and about 3.5 cm (1¹/₂ in) apart.

5. Bake for about 20 minutes, until choux puffs are golden and puffy.

6. In the meantime, prepare chocolate ganache. Heat cream in a saucepan. Once boiling, remove from heat and add chocolate chunks. Let it sit for about 3 minutes before giving it a vigorous stir. Stir in butter to give it a shiny finish. Keep chocolate ganache warm.

7. When choux pastry is ready, sandwich whipped cream between every two puffs. Top with generous drizzles of warm chocolate ganache and serve.

𝒫astries are a great alternative to cakes and taste particularly good with a strong cup of coffee. Choux pastries are commonly served with chocolate, toffee or cheese. I like mine with fresh whipped cream and silky chocolate ganache. The shell is easy to make but requires some elbow grease. The delicate, hollow choux puffs are well worth the hard work and definitely beats lifting weights.

Apple Frangipane Tart

Makes one 20-cm (8-in) tart

Ready-made dough 170 g (6 oz), chilled

Butter for greasing

Apples 5, cored and sliced into wedges

Castor sugar for sprinkling

Apricot jam 4 Tbsp, heated

Toasted almonds 2 Tbsp, chopped

Frangipane

Butter 75 g ($2^2/_3$ oz), softened

Icing (confectioner's) sugar 75 g ($2^2/_3$ oz)

Almond meal 75 g ($2^2/_3$ oz)

Brandy 1 Tbsp

Egg 1

1. Prepare frangipane. Beat butter and sugar in a mixer until pale. Add almond meal, brandy and egg. Continue to beat until well combined. Chill until needed.

2. Preheat oven to 180°C (350°F).

3. Roll out ready-made dough into a round shape, about 5 cm (2 in) bigger than a 20-cm (8-in) fluted cake pan. Gently fit dough into greased cake pan, pressing the base and side such that it sits nicely. Prick dough with a fork. Line the base with greaseproof paper and place baking weights onto the base. Blind bake for 7 minutes. Remove baking weights and continue baking for another 5 minutes to get a nice golden colour.

4. Spread frangipane on the pastry base and arrange apples over it, fanning out the fruit wedges such that they are evenly distributed. Sprinkle castor sugar and dot butter all over to prevent apples from drying out during baking.

5. Bake for about 45 minutes, depending on your oven, until the top is golden brown and tart is cooked through.

6. When tart is done, glaze over with apricot jam and top with toasted almonds.

7. Serve warm or chilled.

Note: Blind baking prevents the pastry from turning soggy. Dried grains such as uncooked rice grains or beans can be baking weights.

I grew up near an apple orchard and loved going there with my mum to pick up bags of fresh, crisp apples. To make the most of the apple season, my mum would bake apple cakes that were moist and sweet from the natural sugars of the fruit. This tart is in memory of those wonderful apple seasons. I love almond paste so I added frangipane for a new spin to a French classic, tarte aux pomme.

Episode 9

What I love about New York is the diversity of its people. With Italians in NoLita, the Chinese community in Flushing and Upper East Side full of Cuban eateries, it's hard not to get lost in all the different neighbourhoods and forget you are in fact in New York. The boroughs beyond SoHo are full of characters that can't be found anywhere else in the world, giving us food lovers a playground of great food destinations.

Beyond SoHo

Creamy Hummus with Crispy Cauliflower

Serves 4

Canned chickpeas 400 g (14 oz), drained

Peanut butter 2 heaped Tbsp

Cumin a pinch

Garlic 2 cloves, peeled and crushed

Lemon juice from 1–2 lemons

Olive oil 3 Tbsp

Water as needed

Salt to taste

Ground black pepper to taste

Roasted Cauliflower

Cauliflower 280 g (10 oz), cut into florets

Olive oil a drizzle

Garlic 3 cloves, peeled and minced

Mix of cumin, sumac and garlic powder 1 tsp

Lemon zest from 1 lemon

Lemon juice from 1/2 lemon

Parsley a few leaves

1. Preheat oven to 220°C (425°F).

2. Prepare roasted cauliflower. Mix all ingredients, except parsley, on a baking tray. Bake for about 25 minutes, until lightly toasted. You may need to turn the cauliflower florets once halfway through to make sure they are evenly browned. Stir in parsley.

3. In the meantime, prepare hummus. Place chickpeas, peanut butter, cumin, garlic and lemon juice in a food processor. As it blends, stream olive oil, followed by just enough water to get a smooth consistency. Season with salt and pepper and scoop onto serving plates.

4. Garnish with roasted cauliflower and serve with warm pita bread.

The hummus gets a smoky makeover with crispy cauliflower, which is baked to impart a roasted flavour to this creamy treat. Enjoy smooth dollops of hummus with warm pita bread. Delicious!

New England Prawn Rolls

Serves 4

Tiger prawns (shrimps) 20, peeled and deveined

Hotdog buns 4, halved

Butter (optional) for spreading

Salad Dressing

Celery 1/2 stalk, finely chopped

Mayonnaise 4 Tbsp

Sour cream 1 Tbsp

Sweet chilli sauce 1 Tbsp

Chives 1 tsp, chopped

Paprika 1/2 tsp

Lemon zest from 1 lemon

Lemon juice fron 1/2 lemon

1. Boil water in a saucepan. When water boils, add prawns. Allow to return to the boil, then remove prawns and immediately plunge into ice-cold water. Drain and refrigerate until needed.

2. Mix all salad dressing ingredients.

3. Cut chilled prawns into bite-size pieces and mix into dressing.

4. Grill hotdog buns and if desired, give a generous spread of butter.

5. Sandwich salad prawns in hotdog buns and serve.

Lobster rolls are hugely popular along the East Coast of the States. To re-create this simple and totally addictive sandwich, all you need is some fresh seafood and a great cream sauce. I like to use prawns instead of lobster because it is more affordable, yet still offers the texture and flavour of the sea in every juicy bite.

Herring and Cabbage Slaw Bagels

Serves 2

Small cabbage ¼ head, finely shredded

Onion 1, peeled and finely sliced

Pickled herring fillets 2, drained

Bagels 2, halved

Butter for spreading

Dressing

Olive oil 4 Tbsp

Tarragon 1 Tbsp, finely chopped

Garlic 1 clove, peeled and minced

Dijon mustard 1 tsp

Lemon juice from 1 lemon

Salt a pinch + more if desired

Ground black pepper a pinch + more if desired

White Vinegar 1 Tbsp + more if desired

1. Combine dressing ingredients to make an emulsion. Adjust salt, pepper and vinegar to taste.

2. Lightly mix cabbage and onion slices. Pour dressing over. Set aside for about 10 minutes until cabbage collapses a little but is still crunchy.

3. Line a baking tray with foil and place the herring fillets skin side up. Grill until the skin is almost charred. Flip if using fresh fillets and make sure they are well cooked.

4. Toast bagels and spread over a generous amount of butter. Top with herring fillets and cabbage slaw.

5. Serve immediately.

There are some great farmers markets in the heart of New York, giving city dwellers a chance to buy local produce. With New York close to the East Coast, fresh seafood is easily available with fishermen setting up stalls alongside other farmers. For this recipe, I prefer to use fresh herrings that I pickle by myself, but for days when I can't do so, good quality store-bought ones work just as well.

Polish Cabbage Rolls

Makes about 12 rolls

Cabbage leaves 12, washed

Ground pork 300 g (10½ oz)

Onion 1, peeled and chopped

Paprika 1 tsp

Worcestershire sauce 1 tsp

Cooked rice 110 g (4 oz)

Salt to taste

Ground black pepper to taste

Egg 1

Water 500 ml (16 fl oz / 2 cups)

Passata 375 ml (12 fl oz / 1½ cups)

1. Blanch cabbage leaves in boiling water for about 2 minutes until they are soft and pliable.

2. Using a sharp knife, remove stems or any parts that are stiff and difficult to fold. Set aside.

3. Mix pork with onion, paprika, Worcestershire sauce and lastly, cooked rice. Season with salt and pepper. Beat egg in and mix well.

4. Spoon about 2 Tbsp meat mixture into the centre of each cabbage leaf. Fold the two sides inwards, then bring the bottom up to cover the meat. Roll upwards to make a secure parcel. Repeat until all ingredients are used up.

5. Arrange cabbage rolls on the bottom of a heavy saucepan. Pour in water, followed by passata.

6. Bring to the boil and simmer for about 1 hour, until meat is cooked through.

7. Serve cabbage rolls piping hot.

Warsaw is one of my favourite Eastern European cities and I was lucky enough to have called it home for two short months. The food, much like the city, was a mix of old and new Warsaw. I enjoyed the creative dishes from chefs, as well as the traditional soups, stews and cakes that share a bit of the country's history in every mouthful. I lived out of my suitcase and dined at restaurants most of the time, but was very lucky to have a friend who shared with me this home-cooked meal, which I hope you will also enjoy.

Portuguese Crème Caramel

Serves 4

Sweetened condensed milk 1 can, about 375 ml (12 fl oz / 1¹/₂ cups)

Evaporated milk 1 can, about 375 ml (12 fl oz / 1¹/₂ cups)

Milk 125 ml (4 fl oz / ¹/₂ cup)

Eggs 3

Vanilla seeds from 1 pod

Orange zest from 1 orange

Caramel

Castor sugar 160 g (5²/₃ oz)

Water 1 Tbsp

1. Preheat oven to 160°C (325°F).

2. Combine caramel ingredients in a pan. Melt sugar over low heat until it becomes a nice toffee colour. This should take about 7 minutes. Don't leave the pan unattended. Do not stir, but swirl occasionally to prevent burning or seizing. Remove from heat and divide among serving ramekins.

3. Whisk ingredients for the custard. Pour into caramel-lined ramekins.

4. Pour boiling water into a deep baking tray to create a water bath. Place ramekins in the water bath and bake for at least 30 minutes. This should give a soft flan. If you prefer a firmer texture, bake for another 5–10 minutes.

5. Leave to cool before refrigerating for at least 3 hours before serving.

6. To serve, place each ramekin in a hot water bath for about 20 seconds. Invert ramekin and tip flan onto a serving plate.

Summer in New York can be hot, sticky and humid, so I try not to spend too much time in my kitchen. I take advantage of the cooler nights in the evening to make this sweet delicate dessert. When chilled overnight, the silky smooth texture and deliciously sweet caramel custard is better than ice-cream on a hot summer day.

Episode 10

Good morning Sunshine

Breakfast … just thinking about it makes me hungry. Coming from Melbourne, where a huge café culture resonates, I constantly seek out places to have my mandatory latte and eggs. Buttered artisan toast with soft poached eggs and crispy bacon is absolutely delicious, but sometimes, special occasions call for something a little more fancy. Special breakfasts can be simple and stress-free. These meals are easy and can be prepared the night before for days that you want to sleep in. Great for breakfast or brunch, they make a great start to your day.

Swiss Oatmeal with Crunchy Almonds and Strawberries

Serves 4

Swiss Oatmeal

Oats 180 g (6^1/$_3$ oz)

Almonds 55 g (2 oz), toasted and chopped

Bran 1 Tbsp

Dates 55 g (2 oz), pitted and chopped

Sultanas 75 g (2^2/$_3$ oz)

Apple 1, cored and grated, unpeeled

Yoghurt 3 Tbsp + more if desired

Milk as needed

Strawberry Compote

Strawberries 150 g (5^1/$_3$ oz)

Raw sugar 1 heaped Tbsp

Water 125 ml (4 fl oz / ^{1}/$_2$ cup)

Mint leaves a few leaves, roughly shredded

Caramel Shards

See page 98.

1. Prepare Swiss Oatmeal the night before. Mix oats, almonds and bran in a glass jar. Add remaining ingredients. The milk should be about 1 cm (^{1}/$_2$ in) above the oats, which will absorb the liquid later on. Give a good stir to mix well. Refrigerate overnight.

2. Prior to serving, prepare strawberry compote. Boil strawberries, sugar and water. Reduce to a simmer until syrup becomes slightly thicker. Stir in mint leaves and leave to cool before refrigerating for about 15 minutes.

3. Spoon strawberry compote into serving glasses. Pour Swiss oatmeal over. Top with more yoghurt if desired.

4. Garnish with caramel shards and serve.

This Swiss oatmeal is also known as Bircher muesli. Fresh ingredients and a good mix of oats and grains give this muesli a creamy texture. Use crushed oats as it gives a smoother consistency over rolled oats. This is perfect with stewed fruits like strawberries and dates.

Chocolate Banana Bread with Mascarpone Honey

Makes a 23 x 13 x 8-cm (9 x 5 x 3-in) loaf

Plain (all-purpose) flour 325 g (11½ oz)

Cocoa powder 2 Tbsp

Bicarbonate of soda 1½ tsp

Baking powder 2 tsp

Salt ½ tsp

Large eggs 3

Brown sugar 200 g (7 oz)

Very ripe bananas 3, mashed

Walnut oil 125 ml (4 fl oz / ½ cup)

Vanilla extract 1 tsp

Walnuts 45 g (1½ oz), roughly chopped + more for topping

Chocolate shavings (optional) 4 Tbsp

Mascarpone Honey

Mascarpone cheese 225 g (8 oz)

Ricotta cheese 45 g (1½ oz)

Honey 2 Tbsp

1. Preheat oven to 180°C (350°F).

2. Whisk together flour, cocoa powder, bicarbonate of soda, baking powder and salt.

3. In a separate bowl, beat eggs and sugar until fluffy. Whisk in mashed bananas, followed by oil. Mix in vanilla extract, walnuts, and chocolate shavings if using. Fold into flour mixture until just combined.

4. Pour batter into a greased loaf pan. Sprinkle over walnut topping and bake for about 1 hour 25 minutes. Check after 1 hour of baking. Test doneness by inserting a skewer into the centre of the loaf. It should come out clean if loaf is done.

5. Meanwhile, mix all ingredients for Mascarpone honey. Serve with chocolate banana bread.

My aunt makes one of the best banana breads in the world. The trick is to use very ripe bananas with sweet sticky flesh. Mascarpone honey goes well with day-old banana bread that is heated up slightly on the grill. I have made this a little more indulgent by adding chocolate and cocoa powder.

Cheesy Herbs and Fish Omelette

Serves 2

Bay leaf 1

Black peppercorns 3

Milk enough to cover fish

Smoked haddock or cod fillet 1

Lemon zest from ½ lemon

Parmesan cheese 2 Tbsp, grated

Salt a pinch

Ground black pepper a pinch

Butter 1 Tbsp

Large eggs 3, beaten

Fresh herbs a generous handful, roughly chopped

1. Heat bay leaf, peppercorns and milk in a pan over medium heat.

2. Place smoked fish fillet into heated milk and poach for 10–12 minutes, until the fish is tender. Set aside to cool. Once cool, flake fish meat and remove any bones.

3. Mix lemon zest and Parmesan cheese. Season with salt and pepper. Set aside.

4. Heat butter in a frying pan. Pour in eggs, then sprinkle flaked fish, followed by chopped herbs.

5. Spoon cheese mixture over the egg, then fold omelette. Remove from heat immediately and serve.

Cooking omelettes can take too much time when using potatoes and other vegetables that require some pre-cooking. For a fresh, flavourful breakfast, I use smoked fish and lots of garden herbs. Fresh greens like parsley or rocket leaves add refreshing flavours to the omelette.

Strawberry Soup

Serves 4

Sugar 2 Tbsp, more if desired

Cardamom pods 2, crushed

Water 375 ml (12 fl oz / 1¹/₂ cups)

Strawberries 450 g (1 lb), washed and stems removed

Lime juice a squeeze

Lime rind a few strands

Ricotta Chocolate

White chocolate 60 g (2 oz)

Ricotta cheese 250 g (9 oz) + more for garnishing

Single (light) cream 125 ml (4 fl oz / ¹/₂ cup), whipped

1. Prepare Ricotta chocolate. Melt white chocolate over simmering water or in a microwave oven. Cool chocolate before mixing in Ricotta cheese. Fold in whipped cream. Refrigerate until needed.

2. Heat sugar, cardamom and water in a saucepan. Allow to simmer until the sugar dissolves. Add strawberries. Cook until strawberries collapse a little and syrup thickens. Add a squeeze of lime juice and remove from heat. Leave to cool before refrigerating.

3. Serve chilled with dollops of Ricotta chocolate and lime rind.

Calling this a soup might stop many people from trying this recipe, but you really must try it. The refreshing combination of fresh strawberries in cool sugary broth is perfect for a hot and humid day. Pillows of Ricotta add richness to the dessert, which goes well with sweet biscotti.

Jam-filled Donuts

Makes 12 donuts

Plain (all-purpose) flour 140 g (5 oz)

Baking powder 1 tsp

Bicarbonate of soda $\frac{1}{2}$ tsp

Salt a pinch

Large eggs 2

Sugar 170 g (6 oz)

Vanilla seeds from 1 pod

Butter 75 g (2$\frac{2}{3}$ oz) + more for coating

Milk 125 ml (4 fl oz / $\frac{1}{2}$ cup)

Buttermilk 125 ml (4 fl oz / $\frac{1}{2}$ cup)

Jam for donut filling

Coating

Sugar 200 g (7 oz)

Ground cinnamon 1$\frac{1}{2}$ tsp

Five-spice and ground cloves mix $\frac{1}{4}$ tsp

1. Preheat oven to 180°C (350°F).

2. Mix together flour, baking powder, bicarbonate of soda and salt. Sift mixture twice.

3. In a separate bowl, beat eggs and add sugar. Whip for about 1 minute, until slightly pale in colour. Beat in vanilla seeds and butter. Sift in half of the flour mixture and mix. Stir in milk and buttermilk, followed by the remaining flour mixture. Stir until just combined, taking care not to overwork the mix.

4. Spoon batter into greased muffin tray until the moulds are half-filled. Drop a small dollop of jam onto each mould of batter and top off with batter until three-quarters full. Bake for about 12 minutes.

5. Meanwhile, mix coating ingredients.

6. When donuts are done, dip in warm butter before coating with sugary spice mix.

Fried donuts dusted with sugar are totally addicitive with a hot cup of coffee. But to make this healthier, I have adapted a regular donut recipe and made it less sinful and more kitchen-friendly. This recipe cuts out any hard work in the kitchen by not using yeast. It also doesn't call for vats of deep-frying oil. Love it!

Episode 11

Eating with Sticks

When it comes to simple meals, I turn to my childhood for inspiration. My mum is the ultimate cook when it comes to churning out delicious food in a matter of minutes. With a few simple ingredients, she can create an awesome dinner. This section contains recipes with strong Asian flavours, from classics to modern twists that even my mum questioned initially, but grew to love later on. All these are simple enough for you to whip up without calling Mum for help.

Spicy Korean Chicken Bites

Serves 4

Cooking oil for stir-frying

Chicken pieces 400 g (14 oz), cut into bite-size pieces

Garlic 2 cloves, peeled and chopped

Korean red spicy sauce 2 heaped Tbsp

Light soy sauce 1 Tbsp

Shaoxing or Huadiao wine 2 Tbsp

Brown sugar 1/2 Tbsp

Water as needed

Coriander a few leaves

Spring onions (scallions) a handful, chopped

Garlic 1 clove, peeled and sliced

1. Heat oil in a pan. Lightly fry chicken pieces until coloured on the outside.

2. Place chicken, garlic, Korean paste, soy sauce, Shaoxing or Huadiao wine, followed by sugar in a deep saucepan. Fill with enough water to cover all ingredients. Bring to the boil and simmer for at least 35 minutes. Stir occasionally. When liquid has reduced and meat is tender, remove from heat. Test doneness by inserting a chopstick into the meat. It should go in easily.

3. Garnish with coriander, spring onions and garlic. Serve with steaming white rice or Chinese steamed buns.

I really love quick braises and this is one of my favourite recipes. This is quick and easy, yet full of flavour. It goes well with steamed white rice, but I prefer to stuff it in Chinese steamed buns.

Spicy Chicken with Kung Pao Punch

Serves 2

Chicken breast 150 g (5⅓ oz), skinned

Cooking oil for stir-frying

Red chillies 5–6, sliced

Garlic 2 cloves, peeled and finely sliced

Fresh ginger 2.5-cm (1-in) knob, peeled and grated

Allspice a sprinkle

Red pepper (capsicum) ½, finely chopped

Spring onion (scallion) 1 stalk, roughly chopped

Toasted peanuts 4 Tbsp

Marinade

Light soy sauce 1 Tbsp

Dry port wine 1 Tbsp

Corn flour (cornstarch) ½ Tbsp

Ground white pepper ½ tsp

Sauce

Light soy sauce 2 Tbsp

Shaoxing, Huadiao wine or dry port 1 Tbsp

Sugar 1 tsp

Black vinegar ¼ tsp

Water 2 Tbsp

1. Rinse chicken under cold water and pat dry with a clean towel. Cut into bite-size pieces. Mix marinade ingredients and pour over the chicken. Refrigerate for 1 hour, or at least 15 minutes if you're pressed for time.

2. Mix sauce ingredients in a bowl and set aside.

3. Heat oil in a large pan. When oil is hot, cook chicken pieces over high heat, moving them around the pan.

4. When chicken pieces have browned, move them to the side and add a bit more oil to the centre of the pan. Add red chillies, garlic and ginger. Sauté for about 1 minute until fragrant. Sprinkle allspice before adding red pepper. Sauté for another minute. Pour in sauce and do a quick stir-fry for another minute, this time mixing in the chicken pieces.

5. When chicken is cooked, garnish with spring onion and peanuts.

6. Serve with freshly steamed rice.

My grandfather's restaurant in Los Angeles is one of the best hole-in-the-wall destinations you can go to for delicious Chinese food. A 42-year-old recipe for dumplings is the house speciality, but the kung pao chicken is just as good. Dry chillies give a kick without numbing the mouth. A second serving of steamed rice is totally justified with this spicy dish.

Jojo's Omelette

Serves 2

Cooking oil for frying

Fresh prawns (shrimps) 100 g (3¹/₂ oz), deveined and cleaned, tails intact

Eggs 3, beaten

Edamame beans 100 g (3¹/₂ oz)

1. Heat oil in a pan. When oil is very hot, cook prawns until they just turn pink. Remove from heat.

2. Add more oil to the pan and pour in eggs. Cook for about 1 minute, lightly scrambling the egg as it firms up. Return prawns to the pan and sprinkle in edamame beans. Turn off the heat and let the residual heat cook the egg awhile more.

3. Serve with steamed white rice.

Eggs may be a breakfast item in the States but in Asia, eggs are often used in simple family-style recipes. This one combines silky eggs with fresh prawns and edamame. My uncle makes the best rendition of this so I hope this meets his standards and makes him happy.

Crunchy Peanut Salad

Serves 2–3

Carrot 1, julienned

Bean sprouts a handful, tails removed

Chinese cabbage 2 handfuls, shredded

Coriander leaves a small handful, coarsely chopped

Lime slices for garnishing

Dressing

Peanut sauce 1 Tbsp

Roasted peanuts 2 Tbsp, crushed + more for tossing

Garlic 3 cloves, peeled

Bird's eye chillies 2

Sugar 1 tsp

Fish sauce 1 tsp

Lime juice from 2 limes + more if needed

1. Mix carrot, bean sprouts and Chinese cabbage together.

2. For the dressing, pound all ingredients with a mortar and pestle. Mix well and drizzle over the vegetables. Add more lime juice if too dry, or a splash of hot water to loosen the salad. Toss with more roasted peanuts.

3. Garnish with coriander and lime slices. Serve.

I tend to go over-the-top when I shop at a farmers market. Garden vegetables straight from the ground and fresh farm eggs encourage me to buy the entire crate or basket. On my last visit, I purchased far too many vegetables and needed new and exciting ways to eat up all my veggies while they were still fresh. Rather than cooking out the flavour and sweetness of my vegetables, I came up with this peanut salad, which doesn't involve any frying. The chillies bring out the flavours of all the ingredients. Serve with grilled vegetables or simply eat it on its own.

Gyoza with Pickled Cucumbers

Makes at least 24 gyozas

Ground pork 150 g (5$^1/_3$ oz)

Ginger 2.5-cm (1-in) knob, peeled and finely grated

Spring onions (scallions) 1 tsp, finely chopped

Cold water 2 Tbsp + more for sealing

Light soy sauce 1 tsp + more for dipping

Fresh prawns (shrimps) 150 g (5$^1/_3$ oz), shelled
　and diced

Cabbage a handful, finely shredded

Gyoza wrappers at least 24

Olive oil for pan-frying

Pickled cucumber

Cucumber 1

Salt to taste

Garlic 2 cloves, peeled and pounded

Red chilli 1, thinly sliced

Vinegar to taste

1. Mix pork with ginger and spring onions. Add cold water and soy sauce, followed by prawns and cabbage. Mix well and refrigerate for about 15 minutes to let it steep in the marinade.

2. Spoon about 2 tsps filling into a gyoza wrapper. Ensure filling is compact before folding the wrapper over. Moisten the edges of the wrapper with some cold water. Seal one end of the gyoza first, then form pleats from the sealed end until filling is securely enclosed. Repeat until pork mix is used up. These dumplings can be kept frozen for about a month.

3. Heat oil a large non-stick pan. When hot, add dumplings. Add enough water so that the liquid is less than halfway up the gyozas. Cover and cook for 10–15 minutes. Once the water has evaporated, continue to cook until the base of of the gyozas turn a golden brown colour.

4. Serve with pickled cucumber and soy sauce.

Pickled Cucumber

1. Wash cucumber and remove alternating strips of peel.

2. Thinly slice cucumber. Sprinkle salt all over and leave in a colander to marinate for about 30 minutes.

3. Rinse off residual salt under cold running water and drain well.

4. Mix cucumber slices with garlic and chilli. Top with vinegar.

5. Let it sit for at least 6 hours, preferably overnight, before serving.

I travel quite a bit, and I usually do a few things before getting settled in a new apartment. One of the few things I'll do is make dumplings. It not only helps me settle in, but dumplings are also great for quick dinners during unpacking and furniture-building projects. I always make my own dough, but for quick dinners, I secretly use store-bought pastry. Using ready-made wrappers in Japan is common so I happily call these gyozas and not dumplings!

Episode 12

Party!

In a city that never sleeps, I feel almost guilty if I don't have a party on a weekly basis. While my nights out on the dance floor are a little more tamed these days, having friends over still makes up most of my weekends. Catching up with friends over chilled cocktails and crowd-pleasing appetisers is my perfect Friday night in SoHo. What could be better than entertaining good friends with good food? Forget bowls of salty chips and frozen snacks nuked in the microwave — these party ideas are hot!

Mini Mushroom and Bacon Quiche

Makes at least 24 mini quiches

Bacon 1 rasher, cut into squares

Eggs 4

Double (heavy) cream 150 ml (5 fl oz)

Sour cream 2 Tbsp

Mushrooms a handful, finely diced

Gruyère or real Cheddar cheese 100 g (3^1/$_2$ oz),
  grated

Large pastry sheets at least 2

1.   Preheat oven to 200°C (400°F).

2.   Fry bacon until crispy. Set aside.

3.   Lightly beat eggs and add fried bacon, double cream and sour cream. Mix before adding mushrooms and grated cheese. Set quiche custard aside.

4.   Roll out pastry sheets. Cut out mini rounds with a pastry cutter or floured rim of a small cup. Fit pastry rounds into greased moulds of a mini muffin tray. Prick the base and edges of the pastry with a fork.

5.   Pour quiche custard into pastry rounds and bake for about 10 minutes, until fluffy and risen.

6.   Serve warm.

*This custard quiche is silky and creamy without being too strong in flavour.
Quick, easy and chic for a party, it's difficult to stop at just one.*

Garlic Chicken Wings

Serves 6–8

Chicken wings 1 kg (2 lb 3 oz)

Marinade
Garlic 5–8 cloves, peeled and chopped
Light soy sauce 3 Tbsp
Oyster sauce 1 Tbsp
Sherry, Port or beer 1 Tbsp
Ground white pepper 1/2 tsp

1. Wash chicken wings under cold running water. Drain well.

2. Mix marinade ingredients in a bowl.

3. Place chicken wings in a clean bag and pour in marinade. Lightly squish the bag to coat chicken wings evenly. Leave to marinate for at least 2 hours.

4. Preheat oven to 180°C (350°F).

5. Line a baking tray with foil and arrange chicken wings over. Reserve leftover marinade sauce.

6. Bake for about 25 minutes, until chicken wings are slightly charred on the outside. Pour leftover marinade over the wings and continue to bake for another 10 minutes, until chicken wings are crusty on the outside.

7. Serve immediately.

All my family BBQs involve a buffet setting with loads of food. Lots of food, yet never any leftovers. Our BBQs are not typical. We have hamburgers topped with a fried egg and beetroot, potato salads with Japanese mayo and of course, garlic chicken wings — sticky and crunchy on the outside yet succulent on the inside. I love the strong garlic marinade that strengthens the flavour of the sauce.

Buttery Sausage Biscuits

Makes 12 biscuits

Sausages 2, casings removed

Plain (all-purpose) flour 150 g (5⅓ oz)

Egg wash 1 egg, beaten

Dry breadcrumbs 100 g (3½ oz)

Cooking oil for frying

Mascarpone Mustard

Mascarpone cheese 110 g (4 oz)

Sweet German mustard 1 Tbsp OR
   Wholegrain mustard 1 Tbsp + 1 tsp honey

Biscuits

Plain (all-purpose) flour 250 g (9 oz)

Salt ½ tsp

Sugar 1 Tbsp

Baking powder 3 tsp

Cold butter 125 g (4½ oz)

Buttermilk 6 Tbsp + more if needed

1. Mould sausage meat into bite-size balls. Dust over with flour, followed by egg wash and lastly breadcrumbs.

2. Heat oil to 180°C (350°F). Lightly fry battered meatballs until golden brown. Remove from heat and drain off oil on a wire rack.

3. Mix ingredients for Mascarpone mustard. Smear onto biscuits and sandwich a meatball in between. Repeat until all meatballs are used up.

4. Serve immediately.

Biscuits

1. Preheat oven to 220°C (425°F).

2. Whisk flour, salt, sugar and baking powder together.

3. Working quickly, combine butter and flour mixture with your fingertips until it resembles coarse breadcrumbs, leaving large chunks of butter marbled within the flour.

4. Add buttermilk and mix to combine. Bring together to form a dough. Add more buttermilk if too dry.

5. Roll out dough until it is about 2 cm (⅘ in) thick. Do not press too hard so that dough remains light.

6. Cut out rounds of dough with a floured cookie cutter and place on a greased baking tray. Refrigerate for about 10 minutes.

7. Bake at the topmost rack for about 10 minutes, until biscuits have risen and are golden brown.

8. Serve with Mascarpone mustard and meatballs.

Note: Sweet Mascarpone mustard is best made with Händlmaier's German mustard, but wholegrain mustard is delicious too. Just add 1 tsp honey to sweeten it up.

This was inspired by a visit to a unique tapas restaurant in Germany. The kitchen was almost as small as mine in New York and so I thought, "If they can make this, so can I!"

Crab Dip and Bagel Chips

Serves 4

Bagels 2
Butter 2 Tbsp, melted

Crab Dip
Sour cream or Greek yoghurt 2 Tbsp
Mayonnaise 2 Tbsp
Lemon juice from 1 lemon
Lemon zest 1/2 tsp
Fresh dill 1 tsp, finely chopped
Small red onion 1, peeled and finely chopped
Chives 1 Tbsp, chopped
Crab meat a handful, shredded
Olive oil 1 tsp
Salt a sprinkle
Ground white pepper a sprinkle

1. Preheat oven to 180°C (350°F).

2. Slice bagels thinly. Brush with butter and bake until golden brown. Flip halfway through so that both sides are nicely toasted. Set aside to cool.

3. Prepare crab dip. Mix all ingredients for crab dip except crab meat, olive oil, salt and pepper. When well-mixed, stir in remaining ingredients.

4. Serve crab dip with crispy bagel chips.

My obsession with bagels led to an overstuffed freezer filled with these lovely donut-shaped bread. I've had nightmares that one day, I will walk into a bagelry to find absolutely no bagels left, so I tend to purchase by the dozen. To use up extra bagels, I make this creamy yet slightly zingy crab dip that goes well with crunchy bagel chips for a quick and tasty party snack.

Mango and Lime Daiquiri

Makes 2 cocktails

Lime zest from 1 lime

Mango 1, peeled and diced

Mint leaves a few

Large ice cubes 2

Plum wine 15 ml ($^1/_2$ fl oz)

Fresh lime juice 30 ml (1 fl oz)

White rum 30 ml (1 fl oz)

Dark rum 30 ml (1 fl oz)

Mango purée 90 ml (3 fl oz)

Lime rind 5-cm (2-in) peel

Sparkling water as needed

1. Divide lime zest, mango and mint leaves between each glass.

2. In a cocktail shaker, combine remaining ingredients, except lime rind and sparkling water. Give a few shakes to break up the ice.

3. Pour over a cocktail strainer into serving glasses.

4. Light a match and hold it between the surface of the drink and the lime rind. With the flame closer to the rind, squeeze the rind a couple of times while flaming it. This gives the cocktail a nice citrusy aroma.

5. Serve immediately with sparkling water for an easier drink.

Parties start well with a fun drink. Rather than just stocking up on beer, I always like to have one signature cocktail to match at least one of my appetisers. This mango and lime cocktail pairs well with buttery quiches. The plum wine adds sweetness, making it dangerously easy to drink. A bartender I met in Portugal shared a secret to get the guests in a party mood — a matchstick and some lime zest.

Weights and Measures

Quantities for this book are given in Metric and American (spoon and cup) measures. Standard spoon and cup measurements used are: 1 tsp = 5 ml, 1 Tbsp = 15 ml, 1 cup = 250 ml. All measures are level unless otherwise stated.

LIQUID AND VOLUME MEASURES

Metric	Imperial	American
5 ml	$^1/_6$ fl oz	1 tsp
10 ml	$^1/_3$ fl oz	1 dsp
15 ml	$^1/_2$ fl oz	1 Tbsp
60 ml	2 fl oz	$^1/_4$ cup (4 Tbsp)
85 ml	2 $^1/_2$ fl oz	$^1/_3$ cup
90 ml	3 fl oz	$^3/_8$ cup (6 Tbsp)
125 ml	4 fl oz	$^1/_2$ cup
180 ml	6 fl oz	$^3/_4$ cup
250 ml	8 fl oz	1 cup
300 ml	10 fl oz ($^1/_2$ pint)	1$^1/_4$ cups
375 ml	12 fl oz	1$^1/_2$ cups
435 ml	14 fl oz	1$^3/_4$ cups
500 ml	16 fl oz	2 cups
625 ml	20 fl oz (1 pint)	2$^1/_2$ cups
750 ml	24 fl oz (1$^1/_5$ pints)	3 cups
1 litre	32 fl oz (1$^3/_5$ pints)	4 cups
1.25 litres	40 fl oz (2 pints)	5 cups
1.5 litres	48 fl oz (2$^2/_5$ pints)	6 cups
2.5 litres	80 fl oz (4 pints)	10 cups

DRY MEASURES

Metric	Imperial
30 grams	1 ounce
45 grams	1$^1/_2$ ounces
55 grams	2 ounces
70 grams	2$^1/_2$ ounces
85 grams	3 ounces
100 grams	3$^1/_2$ ounces
110 grams	4 ounces
125 grams	4$^1/_2$ ounces
140 grams	5 ounces
280 grams	10 ounces
450 grams	16 ounces (1 pound)
500 grams	1 pound, 1$^1/_2$ ounces
700 grams	1$^1/_2$ pounds
800 grams	1$^1/_2$ pounds
1 kilogram	2 pounds, 3 ounces
1.5 kilograms	3 pounds, 4$^1/_2$ ounces
2 kilograms	4 pounds, 6 ounces

LENGTH

Metric	Imperial
0.5 cm	$^1/_4$ inch
1 cm	$^1/_2$ inch
1.5 cm	$^3/_4$ inch
2.5 cm	1 inch

ABBREVIATION

tsp	teaspoon
Tbsp	tablespoon
g	gram
kg	kilogram
ml	millilitre

OVEN TEMPERATURE

	°C	°F	Gas Regulo
Very slow	120	250	1
Slow	150	300	2
Moderately slow	160	325	3
Moderate	180	350	4
Moderately hot	190/200	370/400	5/6
Hot	210/220	410/440	6/7
Very hot	230	450	8
Super hot	250/290	475/550	9/10